Promoting Peace as the Antidote to Violent Extremism

Evaluation of a Philippines-Based Tech Camp and Peace Promotion Fellowship

ASHLEY L. RHOADES, TODD C. HELMUS, JAMES V. MARRONE,
VICTORIA SMITH, ELIZABETH BODINE-BARON

RAND NATIONAL SECURITY RESEARCH DIVISION

For more information on this publication, visit www.rand.org/t/RRA233-3

Library of Congress Cataloging-in-Publication Data is available for this publication.
ISBN: 978-1-9774-0575-3

Published by the RAND Corporation, Santa Monica, Calif.

Cover image: Rifka Hayati / Getty Images

Preface

This report presents the results of a tech camp and Peace Promotion Fellowship (PPF) program implemented by Equal Access International (EAI) in the Philippines. During the two tech camps conducted as part of the program, EAI offered training in social media and community-building to a cadre of civil society activists in Mindanao, the site of a decades-long conflict between Muslim groups and the Philippine government. After the training, 11 activists participated in a six-month Peace Promotion Fellowship program, which offered mentorship and funding for them to implement their own community-based micro–countering violent extremism campaigns. To evaluate the process for this program, RAND Corporation researchers conducted in-depth interviews with the 11 PPF fellows and with the EAI staffers charged with running the program.

This report also contains information on research on EAI's countering violent extremism–themed programming in Mindanao.

In accordance with the appropriate statutes and regulations regarding human subject protection, the researchers used human subject protection protocols for this report and its underlying research. The views represented in this report do not represent the official policy or position of the U.S. Department of State or the U.S. government.

This research was sponsored by the Global Engagement Center at the U.S. Department of State and conducted within the International Security and Defense Policy Center of the RAND National Security Research Division (NSRD), which operates the National Defense Research Institute (NDRI), a federally funded research and development center sponsored by the Office of the Secretary of Defense, the

Joint Staff, the Unified Combatant Commands, the Navy, the Marine Corps, the defense agencies, and the defense intelligence enterprise.

For more information on the RAND International Security and Defense Policy Center, see www.rand.org/nsrd/isdp or contact the director (contact information is provided on the webpage).

Contents

Figures and Tables

Figures

Tables

Summary

The Philippines continues to experience militant violence, much of which is focused on the southern island of Mindanao and the neighboring Sulu archipelago. Equal Access International (EAI) trained local civil society members in Mindanao to design and implement locally based countering violent extremism (CVE) campaigns. This training was provided through two five-day tech camps. EAI then selected 11 activists to participate in a six-month Peace Promotion Fellowship (PPF) program. This program offered mentorship and funding for them to implement their own community-based micro-CVE campaigns.

To evaluate the process of implementing this program, we conducted in-depth interviews with the 11 PPF fellows and the EAI staff who implemented the program. During these interviews, we also asked the PPF fellows about their experiences during the tech camps. Based on the information that we received during these interviews, we provide recommendations for improving future tech camp and PPF programming.

Tech camp participants had the following suggestions:

- Avoid cramming too much content into a single day to increase absorption of material.
- Hold more breakout sessions that are focused on practical application.
- Give more training on project management and implementation.
- Introduce the PPF concept at the start of future tech camps.

PPF fellows and implementers had the following recommendations:

- PPF implementers provide helpful coaching (while outside mentors are sometimes not helpful). PPF should continue its level of coaching; having enough dedicated staff is vital to this effort.

- Fellows often operate in "hard-to-reach" locations (both physically and virtually) and PPF staff may be difficult to contact. Increasing staff can help improve monitoring and oversight for these fellows.
- Implementers should consider competing responsibilities (such as school and work) when designing program requirements.
- Implementers should increase the number of fellows to compensate for anticipated attrition.
- Increased funding would help build and sustain projects.
- Unforeseen circumstances, such as natural disasters and family demands, can significantly disrupt projects. Implementers should assist fellows with contingency planning in advance of project implementation.
- Give fellows more assistance with establishing critical and helpful social networks.
- EAI implementers pointed out that fellows must have credibility with their local communities to be successful messengers. Implementers seem to have selected credible fellows in the first PPF iteration, and they should ensure that their efforts continue.

We conclude by offering recommendations for a more-quantitative assessment of the program's process and evaluating the effects of future tech camp and PPF programming. We note that future evaluations should make better use of assessments of training quality; surveys administered pre- and post-training can help determine whether the training met initial goals. In addition, researchers and implementers should collect available data on participant social media use to gauge participant performance. Finally, we highlight that it would be ideal to assess the effect of the micro-CVE campaigns on target audience attitudes and behavior, although this goal is the most difficult to achieve.

This report also contains information on research that we conducted on EAI's CVE–themed research programming in Mindanao. Because of data quality issues, this information was not published in a separate report.

Acknowledgments

We are grateful to the numerous individuals and entities that supported the conduct of this research. In particular, we are grateful to the staff at Equal Access International, especially Exan Sharief and Ahmed Harris Pangcoga, who were critical partners throughout the course of this research. We also thank Timothy Andrews and Jill Moss at the U.S. Department of State's Global Engagement Center for trusting the RAND Corporation with this work. We especially thank RAND's Becki Herman, who helpfully advised us about models for training effect and fidelity. Finally, we are grateful to Colin Clarke of Carnegie Mellon University and Jennifer Moroney of RAND for their considered critiques of this report. As always, any and all errors in this report are the sole responsibility of the authors.

Abbreviations

ASG	Abu Sayyaf Group
BARMM	Bangsomoro Autonomous Region in Muslim Mindanao
BOL	Bangsomoro Organic Law
COVID-19	coronavirus disease 2019
CVE	countering violent extremism
EAI	Equal Access International
ISIS-Philippines	Islamic State–Philippines
MSPSS	Multidimensional Scale of Perceived Social Support
NPA	New People's Army
PPF	Peace Promotion Fellowship
PTVE	preventing and transforming violent extremism

CHAPTER ONE

Introduction

Extremist and militant violence has plagued the Philippines for decades. Since the formation of the New People's Army (NPA), a militant offshoot of the local Communist party, in the late 1960s, the Philippines has been home to a melee of insurgent and terrorist groups. In addition to the NPA, Islamist groups, such as the Abu Sayyaf Group (ASG), Islamic State–Philippines (ISIS-Philippines), the Maute Group, and others continue to conduct violent attacks. Since 2013, militant groups have conducted between 300 and 400 attacks per year, producing approximately 600 casualties per year (Study of Terrorism and Responses to Terrorism Global Terrorism Database, undated). About one-third of these casualties are caused by Communist and left-wing extremist groups, such as the NPA, and one-third are caused by Islamist militants, such as ISIS and the ASG. The remaining third have unknown perpetrators.

A significant share of this violence occurs in Mindanao and the neighboring Sulu Archipelago.[1] An assortment of militant Islamist groups call Mindanao and the Sulu Archipelago home; they purport to fight on behalf of local Muslims, who make up 23 percent of the Mindanao population (Philippines Statistics Authority, 2017). The violence in Mindanao reached an apex in 2017, when Maute Group rebels—joined by fighters from ISIS-Philippines, the ASG, and other militant groups—seized the city of Marawi. A five-month battle ensued as the Armed Forces Philippines and the Philippine National Police fought

[1] *Mindanao* refers to the second-largest and southernmost island in the Philippines and some of the much smaller islands surrounding it.

to liberate the city. By the end of the battle, over 1,000 people, mostly militants, were killed (Villamor, 2017).

Given the continuing violence, the Philippine government and the international community have engaged in significant efforts to counter extremist violence. One recent initiative was conducted by Equal Access International (EAI), a nonprofit organization that seeks to "drive sustainable and transformative change . . . through participatory media, technology and outreach" (EAI, undated a). EAI worked to empower civil society actors in Mindanao to counter violent extremism in their own communities. EAI selected 30 Filipino activists from a pool of local applicants to attend two week-long tech camps. These tech camps provided training on social media messaging, countering violent extremism (CVE) programming, and community leadership. These two tech camps were held in April and August 2019.

EAI selected 11 graduates of these tech camps and offered funding and continued mentorship through the Peace Promotion Fellowship (PPF) program. These 11 fellows then launched their own six-month micro-CVE campaigns.

In this report, we offer a qualitative assessment of EAI's tech camp and PPF programming. This study was funded by the Global Engagement Center, an interagency entity housed at the U.S. Department of State.

Countering Violent Extremism Through Tech Camp Programming

EAI's initiative is not the first CVE effort to involve tech camp trainings or PPF-like programming. In 2012, the U.S. Department of State funded the Viral Peace program, which trained civil society to share CVE content on social media (Ackerman, 2012). The Department of State then developed the Peer to Peer program. This effort, now funded by Facebook, seeks to engage university students around the world in a competition in which students create online and offline campaigns that challenge hateful and extremist narratives (Facebook, undated).[2] More than 600 Peer to Peer programs have been implemented in the United States and 75 other countries (EdVenture Partners, undated).

A key assumption of such programming is that local civil society actors are more credible than government agents when they communicate CVE messages. Such actors also might have knowledge of local conditions that breed extremism and a better understanding of the needs, wants, and perspectives of their communities. Training and funding could empower these activists to leverage that credibility and local knowledge to effectively undermine extremism through their local influence (Helmus and Bodine-Baron, 2017).

The aims of this CVE programming are similar to those of the commercial influencer model of *brand ambassadorship*. In this model, businesses work to identify and build relationships with local consumers of their brands, then train them and provide support for brand ambassadors to speak about brands in their community and on social media channels.[3] The difference is that local civil society actors are supported to work against extremism, not for a product.

Our Evaluation Strategies

We chose to evaluate EAI's programming in the Philippines using the Kirkpatrick evaluation model, a well-known model originally developed in 1959 to evaluate training programs. The Kirkpatrick model has four levels of evaluation: reaction, learning, behavior, and results (see Figure 1.1).

Level 1 involves understanding learner reactions to the program, such as opinions on training content, materials, instructors, facilities, and delivery methods. As Reio et al. (2017) caveat, positive reactions

2 For further discussion of the Peer to Peer program and its effectiveness, see Jackson et al., 2019.

3 For more information on such programs and their implications for CVE campaigns, see Helmus and Bodine-Baron, 2017.

Figure 1.1
Kirkpatrick's Four-Level Training Evaluation Model

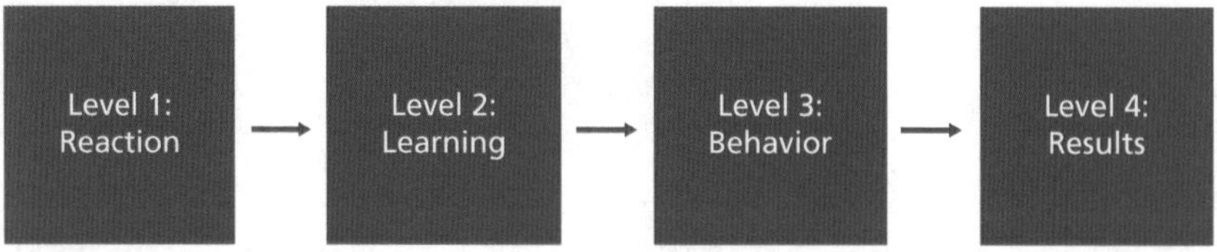

SOURCE: Reio et al., 2017.

do not necessarily mean that participants learned the intended lessons or improved performance.

Level 2 involves assessing whether participants learned the intended lessons from the training program. During Level 2 assessment, evaluators identify specific changes in attitudes, knowledge, and skills. However, Level 2 assessment does not involve measuring improvement in performance.

Level 3 involves performance assessment—whether the training improved participants' ability to apply their knowledge and skills on the job.

Finally, Level 4 involves examining the degree to which training improved institutional or organizational experiences. These experiences could include improved sales, lower turnover, decreased costs, or increased production.

The Kirkpatrick evaluation model does not line up perfectly with tech camp and PPF-type training, especially in terms of Level 4 (results). EAI's efforts are expected to have indirect effects. Program participants would use their training to engage in micro-CVE campaigns, which would, in turn, affect these microcampaigns' audiences. Measuring program results would, therefore, not involve assessing the training attendees themselves, but rather assessing changes in the attitudes and behaviors of their audiences. Such assessments are feasible with a focus on one specific micro-CVE campaign. This was the approach of Savoia et al. (2019), who examined the effects of a single

Peer to Peer CVE campaign implemented in eighth- and ninth-grade classrooms in Utah.[4]

However, EAI's programming was meant to produce multiple micro-CVE campaigns. We have argued that tech camps should allow individual participants to develop and implement unique programs that reflect their interests. This helps participants remain engaged with their efforts and better communicate with their specific audiences (Helmus and Bodine-Baron, 2017). This approach often results in several sets of interventions, each with a unique set of activities and goals. This diversity might aid with engagement and communication, but it does prohibit traditional assessments, such as opinion poll surveys performed before and after programming, because there is no one set of uniform outcome measures from a tech camp. Consequently, we were unable to conduct Level 4 evaluation of EAI's programming.

We also considered approaches to performance (Level 3), such as measuring whether training and support increased the degree to which participants increased their use of social media or increased the use of CVE themes on social media. However, performing this assessment was complicated by two factors. First, Mindanao social media users mainly use Facebook;[5] because of Facebook's privacy restrictions, it would be necessary for us to "friend" each participant to determine increased performance, which would pose privacy and human-subjects protections issues. Second, there was no control group against which to measure treatment effects. We considered creating a control group from activists who were waitlisted for the EAI training, but we were told that a comparable group of waitlisted individuals was unavailable.

---

[4] The program, Kombat with Kindness, sought to promote acceptance toward diversity and "fight" hatred with kindness. The authors used two schools with similar socioeconomic and ethnocultural characteristics as control sites. The authors documented mixed effects: Although the campaign did not increase exposure to positive messages in the school, it did decrease exposure to hate messages. In addition, exposure to positive messaging did not produce changes in two key measures of acceptance of ethnocultural diversity (Savoia et al., 2019).

[5] Approximately 75 million Filipinos (out of an estimated population of 107 million) use Facebook. In contrast, about 5.1 million Filipinos use Twitter ("Social Media Statistics in the Philippines," undated).

We did attempt to assess the training at Level 2 (learning). We administered pre- and post-training surveys in both the first and second tech camps. These surveys included a multiple-choice quiz to assess post-training changes in knowledge acquisition, a subjective measure of self-confidence in various skills addressed by the training, and a measure that assessed the degree of social support that participants derived from the relationships that they built with fellow participants. We collected pre- and post-training surveys from the participants in the first tech camp, but problems with collecting an adequate number of post-training surveys marred data collection for the second tech camp. Given these challenges, we present the data on knowledge, self-confidence, and social support for only the first tech camp; this information, together with Level 1 measures (satisfaction in training), is presented in Appendix B.

Approach

Given the challenges in designing a more complex evaluation design, we chose to conduct a process evaluation that relied on semistructured interviews with PPF fellows and relevant EAI staff. We also conducted face-to-face interviews with the 11 PPF fellows at the conclusion of their fellowship. These interviews were mostly used to collect information at Level 1 (reactions to training and mentorship) of the Kirkpatrick model. Through gathering participant reactions, we were able to identify recommendations for improving future tech camp and PPF programming. However, as stated earlier, we do not identify whether the training led to successful micro-CVE programs (Level 4), improved participant performance (Level 3), or improved participant learning (Level 2), although Appendix B addresses participant learning for one of the tech camps.

The interviews took place during a major peace promotion conference held by EAI in the city of Cagayan de Oro, Mindanao. We also conducted interviews with the EAI staff—both those at EAI headquarters in Washington, D.C., and those in the Philippines—who designed and implemented the tech camp and PPF program. The instruments used for interviews with the PPF fellows and EAI staff can be found in Appendix A.

About This Report

In Chapter Two, we present participant perspectives on tech camp training. In Chapter Three, we follow with perspectives of the Peace Promotion Fellowship. In Chapter Four, we provide recommendations for improving future such endeavors. Appendixes A, B, and C provide information on our questionnaire, results from a survey of tech camp participants, and a review of each PPF fellow's micro-CVE campaign.

Appendix D contains information on research that we conducted on EAI's CVE–themed radio programming broadcast in Mindanao. Because of data quality issues, this information was not published in a separate report.

CHAPTER TWO

Tech Camp Assessment

EAI's two tech camps were held in the Philippines in April and August 2019. To evaluate the effects of the April tech camp, we administered pre- and post-training surveys to the 30 participants. In addition, we interviewed the 11 PPF fellows (who had been selected from the pool of tech camp participants) at the culminating event for the PPF program (the January 30–February 1, 2020 OURmindaNOW Summit in Cagayan de Oro, Mindanao). We interviewed the fellows about their peace promotion projects and their experience at the tech camps to assess attitudes and perceptions about their training and the degree to which the tech camps prepared participants for their current CVE efforts.

The first tech camp was held over a period of five eight-hour days at a resort in northern Mindanao in April 2019. A follow-on tech camp took place in August 2019. Table 2.1 lists the key themes addressed in the training. The training was structured so that one theme was

Table 2.1
Themes Addressed in the Five-Day Tech Camp Training

Themes	Details
Theme 1	CVE empowerment and leadership
Theme 2	Social media, building audiences, and cybersecurity
Theme 3	Becoming an influencer
Theme 4	Skills and tools to amplify participant voices
Theme 5	Building and implementing a plan, networking, and collaboration

addressed per day (so Theme 1 was addressed on Day 1, Theme 2 on Day 2, etc.) EAI used a mix of lectures and group activities to convey each theme.

How Participants Reacted to Training

Interviewees were largely satisfied with their tech camp experiences. They especially enjoyed the quality of the facilitators and the quality of the curriculum. Participants also noted specific aspects of their tech camps that they felt were implemented particularly well.

Tech Camps Helped with Knowledge of Fundamental CVE Concepts

Nearly all the interviewed tech camp participants stated that they had found the curriculum to be well designed and well taught. Several participants said that it had been their first time encountering the concepts of violent extremism and peace promotion; they felt that they had learned a great deal about the fundamentals of CVE and the drivers of radicalism. Many participants shared that the aspect they found the most helpful was the overview of the history of conflict in Mindanao, including information about the *tri-people* of Mindanao (the Christian, Muslim, and indigenous *Lumad* people of the region). They noted that this history is not taught in schools (it is unclear why this is the case), so they had previously been completely unaware of such issues. Participants also spoke highly of the guest speakers selected to deliver the modules, with one interviewee noting that the guest speakers had "a lot of personality, were very engaging, and were excellent models for public speaking."

Participants Felt They Were Trained in Useful Skills

Participants indicated that they had learned a great deal about digital and social media skills and strategies, as well as public speaking and communication skills. All interviewees stated that they had gained in-depth knowledge about digital and social media strategies and had acquired skills in effectively using social media for CVE campaigns. Participants said that they had learned specific skills, such as videography, photography, and creating radio programs and podcasts. They also stated they had learned how to spot unreliable news sources, use graphics and infographics on social media to effectively create CVE content, and use storytelling to convey and disseminate CVE narratives. Participants also stated that they had increased their public speaking and leadership skills, with one interviewee saying that "I've always been a very shy person, but the tech camp gave me the confidence to speak and the confidence to be a leader in my community."

Participants Felt Tech Camps Encouraged Personal Development and Growth

In addition to practical skills, the tech camp environment fostered personal development and growth among participants. One interviewee stated, "I learned things from the tech camp that I can apply to my daily life, such as how to handle stress and how to see things positively." Others shared that the tech camp sessions had helped them realize that they can be forces for change and for peace in their communities, or, in other words, "influencers of peace." Interviewees expressed that the tech camp had taught them to "open their minds" and to accept "responsibility for spreading peace in [their respective] communities." As one interviewee reflected, "The tech camp taught me how to find peace within myself and share it with my community."

Participants Enjoyed a High Level of Guidance and Support

Several interviewees remarked that the tech camp aspect that they liked the most was the high quality of the facilitators and the other staff directing the training. The participants noted that the staff were engaging, available, and dedicated to ensuring that everyone was included and felt comfortable participating. They also noted that the staff were excellent mentors and provided ample guidance. One interviewee summed up this experience:

> EAI guided me every step of the way throughout the tech camp and the PPF journey. My peace promotion project was born because of them. I was able to achieve everything I have during the tech camp and after [during my fellowship] because of them.

Participants Praised the Open and Collaborative Environment

Several participants also appreciated the open tech camp environment, stating that it encouraged them to freely express their views and perspectives and to hear alternate opinions. Participants emphasized that everyone had an opportunity to express their personal views and stories related to experiences with conflict or extremism. They also enjoyed meeting new people and having a forum to share ideas. Participants found significant value in the level of interaction among participants and the ability to collaborate on project ideas. One interviewee noted that it was particularly useful to make connections with other people from the same region to form a network for future projects while having the opportunity to learn about different cultures and exchange ideas with people from different regions. Participants also appreciated the chance to network with the guest speakers. The majority of participants conveyed that they had found the tech camp environment to be inspirational; as one participant stated, it "gathered lots of young people together and gave us the chance to really work together and motivate one another."

What Participants Learned

Overall, interviewees felt that what they learned prepared them well for the peace promotion projects that they completed as part of the subsequent fellowships. Five participants gave a score of five (with five being the highest score) for how well the tech camp prepared them for their EAI projects. Four participants gave a score of four, and two participants gave a score of 4.5.

Participants' descriptions of tech camp projects primarily reflected with what they stated that they learned during the tech camp, with one interviewee stating that "[t]he training from the tech camp was very effective, and I have taken everything I learned at the camp and applied it to the PPF."

Participants identified a few ways in which the tech camp helped them prepare their projects and improve their own personal development.

Learning to Leverage Social Media in Support of CVE Campaigns

Participants noted that social media skill training (e.g., crafting effective narratives through posts, creating appealing content, basic information on using social media platforms) was one of the most valuable takeaways from the tech camps. The majority of participants indicated that the tech camps had prepared them well for their CVE projects.

Learning Public Speaking and Communication Skills

Most of the interviewed participants also shared that their tech camp equipped them with the public speaking and communication (e.g., delivering elevator pitches) skills needed to effectively implement their projects. Several stated that these skills translated into an increase in their overall self-confidence level.

Learning to Engage in Future CVE Efforts

On a more personal level, multiple interviewees noted that attending a tech camp had instilled a passion for CVE in them and inspired them to engage in CVE efforts in the future, even beyond their fellowships. As one interviewee stated, "The tech camp sparked an interest in peace and countering violent extremism in me, and fueled my passion for peace and advocacy."

Suggestions for Improvement

Interviewees did provide several suggestions for areas of improvement when asked in the course of our interviews. We synthesized the suggestions from the interviews into the following recommendations for how to better structure future tech camps.

Avoid Cramming Too Much Content into a Single Day

The most common feedback from the participants we interviewed was that the tech camp implementers attempted to cram too much material into each day. Participants noted that several sessions were back-to-back, making it difficult to absorb details because "most participants are young, in their early twenties, and have short attention spans."

Others said that the amount of content packed into each day did not give them enough time for planning and reflection. One participant, who also attended the second tech camp in August 2019 as a facilitator, stated that EAI had taken this feedback into consideration and modified the schedule to allow more breaks and a less-compressed agenda.

Include More Breakout Sessions Focused on Practical Application

Participants also suggested breaking up the lectures and training with practical breakout sessions; this would afford participants more time to practice what they learned and to demonstrate to peers and instructors that they had acquired the necessary skill sets. Some participants suggested that implementers should make a point of mixing up groups more frequently during these breakout sessions to ensure that participants get a chance to work with different people.

Provide More Training on Project Management and Implementation

Participants requested that tech camp training include more guidance on day-to-day project implementation in advance of the PPF itself (all interviewees had attended both a tech camp and the PPF). This would include more guidance on logistical issues, such as managing funds for new projects and how establishing community partnerships and networks.

Introduce the Peace Promotion Fellowship Concept at the Beginning of Tech Camps

Program implementers were not able to share details of the PPF with the April 2019 tech camp participants because the PPF program in the Philippines had not yet been fully developed. A few interviewees (who were recruited to the PPF from the April 2019 tech camp) felt that they would have been better prepared had the PPF concept been introduced at the beginning of that tech camp session. This would have allowed them to be in the proper mindset during their tech camp training and to think of questions and topics that might apply to their future projects. Furthermore, not introducing the PPF might have kept some participants from applying to the PPF in the first place. One interviewee shared the following thoughts:

> During the tech camp, I didn't know they would have the [PPF]; it would be good to know this in advance. Then I would have had have more time to consider applying. We were the very first batch of tech camp participants, so we weren't aware of the PPF, and this was the reason not a lot of us were able to apply. We weren't prepared and had not planned around our school schedule, and most of us are university students, so it would help to know about the PPF opportunity sooner.

Overall, the interviewed participants found the tech camps to be valuable experiences that greatly helped them in their peace promotion fellowships. Implementing these rather minor suggested changes could improve the experience and make it even more effective.

CHAPTER THREE

Peace Promotion Fellowship Assessment

As part of its CVE efforts in the Philippines, EAI implemented the PPF, a program designed to provide a select group of participants with the funds and skills necessary to implement projects to promote peace in their respective communities. The program implementers selected 11 participants from the April and August 2019 tech camps to complete six-month peace promotion fellowships that began in August 2019. We interviewed the 11 PPF fellows at the culminating event for the PPF program, the OURmindaNOW Summit held from January 30–February 1, 2020 in Cagayan de Oro, Mindanao. We draw on the insights shared by the PPF fellows in these interviews to provide recommendations for future PPF programming. (For more information about the specific programs created by PPF fellows, see Appendix C.)

Overview of the Peace Promotion Projects

As described by one of the program implementers at EAI, the PPF is a program that focuses on the

> information environment in a particular conflict setting where violent extremism is growing, and looks for ways to create a parallel network or ecosystem that rivals the size and scope of malign actors to counter issues like fake news and violent extremist propaganda. To do this, we adopt what we call an eco-systemic approach which incorporates traditional media, social media,

> television, and audiovisual elements, but really also mobilizes a network of influencers who are credible, trusted, strategic messengers operating in different languages attached to different messaging hubs and who are trained to be offline and online influencers that can create alternative narratives about what youth can and should be doing to create positive social change.

The peace promotion projects were the core of the PPF program, in which the fellows built upon the skills they learned from the tech camp to implement a variety of projects designed to promote peace in selected communities across Mindanao.

Programmatic Support Provided to Peace Promotion Fellows

The PPF program was divided into two phases. During the first three months, fellows focused on researching, planning, and developing their project to ensure that it was appropriately tailored to the issue and community they selected. During the final three months, fellows implemented the plan. The PPF program implementers provided the fellows with various types of training and support throughout the fellowship (see Table 3.1).

Implementers' Goals and Objectives for PPF Program

According to information provided by program implementers, the goals of the PPF program were to

> - [r]aise awareness of Peace Promotion Fellows on peacebuilding and Preventing and Transforming Violent Extremism (PTVE) at the global, national and local levels;
> - [b]uild and sharpen fellows' skills in advocacy development, and project management of communication solutions in communities to promote peacebuilding and PTVE;
> - [u]nderstand community initiatives on PTVE while integrating fellows' skills to develop, manage and evaluate their innovative peace community projects related to their choice of practice area;
> - [p]rovide a venue for mentorship of the peace fellows and receive guidance, support, and motivation from leaders and

Table 3.1
Summary of Training and Support Provided to Peace Promotion Fellowship Fellows

Training	Support
PPF orientation • project planning and consultation • public speaking and pitching ideas • basics of project management • basics of developing advocacies • basics of monitoring and evaluation Webinars and *Bondingan* ("bonding") sessions • online learning • effective project management tools and techniques • power of narratives • partnerships for development • implementing gender-responsive and inclusive projects • recognizing burnout and getting motivated OURmindaNOW Summit (the culminating event of the PPF) • public pitching • processing and reflection sessions • additional training sessions from guest speakers on such topics as how to scale up projects	Mentoring • Staff connected fellows with local mentors with expertise on their selected topic; fellows attended structured mentoring meetings on monthly basis. • Fellows volunteered with the host organization where their mentor works to gain practical experience on peacebuilding or development work. Coaching • Each fellow was assigned to a member of EAI staff as a coach. • Coaching sessions were less structured than mentoring sessions and largely consisted of free-flowing conversations in which fellows could ask EAI staff for help on any questions or issues they had. Networking • Fellows were connected to EAI's seven Messaging Hub regional nodes across the Philippines. • EAI staff connected fellows to possible funders and helped them pitch projects. Funding • Fellows were provided with 40,000 Philippine pesos ($821) in seed funding, disbursed in three installments of 10,000 Philippine pesos, 10,000 Philippine pesos, and 15,000 Philippine pesos over the three-month implementation phase of the project.

SOURCE: Interviews conducted with EAI staff.

field experts in peacebuilding, project management, and media communication;

- [c]reate a community of peace influencers in Mindanao actively promoting positive social change and innovative grassroots solutions.[1]

Objectives and Target Audience of Peace Promotion Projects

Each project was structured differently and involved different activities, but many projects pursued similar objectives. These objectives included raising awareness about conflict and paths to peace in Mindanao, promoting cultural and religious unity, and using education as a means to improve people's livelihoods. In selecting their project topics, the fellows noted that they all picked missions that were of personal importance to them; all but two chose to implement projects close to their homes. Objectives were largely tied to provoking change at a community level.

The main objective of several projects was to teach members of the target community about ongoing conflict in Mindanao and help them understand the concept of peace and the role they could play in promoting it. One fellow stated that the "In the Loop" project, for instance, was

> about addressing the lack of awareness that Davao students have about violent extremism and terrorism; Davao is dubbed the "safest city in Mindanao," but lots of conflicts happen peripherally and we don't hear about it in the media.

This fellow stated that the primary objective of In the Loop was to "produce more advocates for peace in Davao." Another project, called *Pag Iskul Ha*, involved teaching children in an evacuation center about the concept of peace with the hope that "no one ever has to conduct another project like this, where women and children are living in a tent while their fathers or relatives are joining extremist groups out of desperation." The goals of this project were to educate at-risk children, teach them about peace, and develop their personalities in a way

---

[1] These goals were stated in unpublished documents provided by the EAI staff.

that discourages violent behavior. Taking a slightly different approach, the *Pagmata* project involved radio programs covering different CVE-related topics, with the intent of giving parents tools to teach their children about peace and create "active participants in promoting peace in the community, so eventually we can build a society that is tolerant, understanding, and values peace." Indeed, the overarching objective for many of these projects is, as one fellow noted, simply to "promote a culture of peace and to create a generation of peace influencers."

Other projects aimed to promote cultural and religious sensitivity and dispel harmful stereotypes about communities or religious groups in Mindanao, particularly indigenous peoples and the Muslim population. One fellow noted that the general public in Mindanao was generally unfamiliar with indigenous people, which contributes to the isolation and underdevelopment of indigenous communities. Recognizing that "the main reason why some people radicalize is the lack of access, education, and opportunities," this project, *BukidKnown*, seeks to "erase the negative stereotypes about the [indigenous] community; ensure [indigenous people] have roads, healthcare, and other needed infrastructure; open up [indigenous] communities to tourism as a source of revenue; and empower the [indigenous] community with a voice." Another fellow realized that the history of the tri-people of Mindanao was not taught in basic education and formulated a project called *Balik Lantaw* to "promote awareness, understanding, and respect of the Muslims and [indigenous people] to halt the ethnocentrism and ethnic violence happening throughout Mindanao." Similarly, another project, Teen Trail for Peace, relied on intercultural and interreligious exchanges to

> help participants understand the need for cultural sensitivity for one another; teach them to design their own social media campaigns about cultural and social sensitivity; and amplify the voice of peace advocators.

Finally, some projects sought to use education as a means to change the living conditions of certain communities. Most notably, one project, Project *Edukasyon* 2030, endeavored to teach people in remote areas about the United Nations Educational, Scientific and Cultural Organisation 2030 Agenda for Sustainable Development goals to create a "change of behavior in the community and turn knowledge into action," resulting in improved quality of life and reducing the risk that environmental issues could drive radicalization.

The target audience for most projects was youth in various communities; some projects also targeted other groups that could be considered vulnerable to radicalization. Within the broader category of youth, several projects focused specifically on students, ranging from elementary to university level. One interviewee explained the tendency to focus on youth, stating that the "youth in the community are not really attuned to violent extremism and they can be prone to engaging in it if they do not have a sense of belongingness in their community." Another project's target audience included parents as well as their children, reasoning that "children are vulnerable and parents are instrumental in passing on important knowledge—such as red flags for radicalization—to their children." In a similar vein, another project targeted teachers because they are natural vectors for passing knowledge to students and others in the community. Other projects involved leaders of *barangays* (the smallest Philippine administrative units), church groups, and representatives of the Muslim and indigenous communities.

Activities and Outputs of Peace Promotion Projects

The peace promotion projects included a wide variety of activities related to art and culture, education and training, the environment, community engagement, and development. Several projects had a social media component; most fellows used Facebook as their primary platform. Other projects relied more on such in-person events as workshops, community gatherings, and training sessions.

Projects varied greatly in their online reach. Fellows reported reaching anywhere from 600 to 46,700 individuals through social media outlets and receiving anywhere from 200 to 400 likes on their Facebook pages. Beyond disseminating content on social media, outputs primarily consisted of people trained (four to 42, depending on the project) and volunteers recruited (three to 29, depending on the project). Fellows reported engaging face-to-face with 13 to 500 people through their initiatives.

Evaluation of the Peace Promotion Projects

Although several fellows noted that their projects had not been going on long enough to see substantial results, they did share the metrics that they used to gauge success and the observed effect of their projects thus far.

Metrics for Success

Fellows were encouraged to engage in consistent project monitoring and evaluation because they had to submit weekly and monthly progress reports to PPF program implementers. They used several methods for tracking the success of their projects. For example, the In the Loop project requested open-ended testimonials from participating students on how they felt the project had improved their understanding of peace and cultural appreciation. The *Pag Iskul Ha* project relied on observation to judge success, attempting to detect changes in young students' behavior and attentiveness in class, with the plan of testing their reading comprehension at the end of the course. However, the fellow implementing this project noted that the wide age range of the students (from eight to 12) made it difficult to control for variables. Similarly, Project *Edukasyon* 2030 observed whether the target community had made any changes to its environmental policies to determine how successful the project had been. The *BukidKnown* project distributed quizzes to test participants' knowledge about indigenous communities before and after participating in the program. The creator of *Pagmata* used social media activity to assess the "buzz" generated by the radio show produced as part of the product, noting that "if people are talking about the show and passing the message onto others, then the project has been a success." Both the Bangsamoro Youth Peacebuilding and PEACEsonality projects involved models in which participants would rate their confidence on certain variables before the sessions, then rate themselves on the same factors after completing the sessions. The

Bangsamoro Youth Peacebuilding project also held an assessment after each session to identify what went wrong and what went well. Several interviewees said that they used informal measures, such as soliciting feedback from the target community or volunteers during meetings or noting how many new volunteers attended after project events.

Effects

As previously mentioned, although most fellows felt that it was difficult to measure the effects of their programs with fidelity because the projects were fairly short in duration, they did identify several successes. One interviewee, whose project, *BukidKnown*, had focused on establishing tourism as a means of improving the quality of life and reputation of indigenous communities, noted that the indigenous communities had started to become less insular and to welcome visitors from nonindigenous communities. Another felt that the In the Loop project had been a success because it gave students a medium to process and discuss violent extremism through art, saying that

> [a]rt helps people express and approach this conversation in [a] sensitive way. I asked the students to write poems about what they think about issues such as the recent incident where the paramilitary was harassing indigenous people who were displaced because of conflict happening in their area in the mountains. The poems the students submitted may not be worthy of a Nobel Peace Prize for literature, but they were able to express a difficult conversation through art, which has really resonated with other people.
>
> Several interviewees reported a visible improvement in their target community's awareness and understanding of issues surrounding violent extremism. For instance, the creator of the Bangsamoro Youth Peacebuilding project observed that "I have seen first-hand a behavioral change in the young leaders we have trained as part of my project. They have been able to overcome their fears and now have the self-esteem and confidence to be advocates for peace." Others said they had also experienced a significant surge in volunteers over the course of their respective projects, which they saw as a reflection of increased community engagement. The creator of the Teen Trail for Peace project noted that there had

> already been some progress in breaking down barriers between different cultures in Mindanao.
>
> While my project is still starting out, I have already noticed how the intercultural exchanges have been working. People really are willing to get to know each other, and the impact of the program really validates that. If you can learn to respect one another regardless of who you are or where you came from or what religious background you may have, there would be no conflict. That's the biggest impact of my project so far.

In many cases, these projects were the first of their kind in their communities, which some of the fellows saw as successes in their own right. According to the creator of the *Balik Lantaw* project,

> The biggest impact of my project is that it is the first time my municipality has ever had a project of this kind. I have been able to show the local government that peace advocacy is important in Mindanao, particularly in a time where some believe there is peace simply because they haven't seen any war. This project has allowed people to understand the root causes of conflict in Mindanao and how to prevent it in future.

Others felt that their projects had helped Mindanao's image with the rest of the Philippines and international community. For instance, the creator of the *BangsaKulToura* project reflected that "[t]he biggest impact of my project is that I have been able to start showing the world that Mindanao isn't a bad place; it is full of different cultures and natural beauty and it is somewhere you can for the most part visit safely."

Fellows' Opinions of the Program

The fellows found the overall experience of the PPF very rewarding and believed that they had been able to affect their communities, even if in immeasurable or intangible ways. Reflecting on the experience, the fellow who created *Pagmata* stated that

> I'm creating a legacy for myself on my island where there are deep scars and a need for youth advocates. I realized I'm the only one who is advocating for peace on the island; so many people lack empathy for those who are experiencing conflict on other side of Mindanao; this is what fuels me and motivates me at night.

The fellow behind the PEACEsonality project similarly shared, "The students I have helped through this project have given me a purpose in life. Seeing them successful and happy feels very rewarding; I view them as my trophies and feel I have found my purpose in life."

Implementers' Opinions of the Program

The PPF program implementers shared that, from their perspectives, the main success of the PPF program was that it allowed fellows to engage in experiential learning. As a program implementer explained,

> [t]he whole process of learning something by theory, implementing it on the ground, and unlocking lessons and realizations through reflection is one key success of the program. It allowed fellows to see past themselves but also to learn from their co-fellows and the community.

One of the PPF program implementers also remarked that the program, as a whole, largely succeeded because of the initiative of the tech camp participants and fellows themselves, as well as the innovative approach that EAI took to peace promotion. According to this program implementer,

> A lot of the participants took initiative to conduct step-down trainings or re-echo seminars, training hundreds of other youth that weren't captured in reports or indicators, all based on their own initiative. So I think the program had a positive norms change and really helped to bolster citizen engagement and volunteerism. We were able to create different dialogues around the humanization of radicalization. We were able to add more nuance instead of just stigmatizing combatants and show that creating a

> context for rehabilitation is possible. We were talking to [radicalized individuals], featuring them, talking about their stories, and taking peace education in a direction that includes frank discussions about radicalization and violent extremism, which are still very dynamic issues in the Philippines.

From program implementers' perspectives, PPF in the Philippines was a success primarily because it (1) galvanized a community of interest in CVE, formed by the original participants in the tech camp and those that they trained of their own accord and (2) adopted an approach that allowed candid discussions of CVE-related issues. This candid approach allowed inclusion rather than ostracization of those most at risk of radicalization and those who had already fallen prey to radical ideology. Through this inclusion, EAI was able to reach the audience who would benefit most from its CVE programming.

Although the six-month fellowship terms officially ended in January 2020, fellows have reportedly continued with their projects as much as possible and have even used their social media platforms and following cultivated through their projects to assist with coronavirus disease 2019 (COVID-19) messaging efforts. During lockdown in the Philippines, the fellows participated in a social media challenge to provide more reliable, nuanced information on COVID-19 to their communities by sharing content in local languages on the Facebook platforms that they had built as part of their projects. According to the PPF program implementers, although this was an unintended output of the program, the fellows were "very willing to participate in this effort because the saw the opportunity and need for it."

Lessons Learned for Future PPF Programs

During interviews, fellows expressed satisfaction with the support that they had received from the PPF program implementers and shared other elements of the program that they believed had worked well. The fellows also provided feedback on recommendations for improvements to future iterations of the fellowship. We also conducted interviews with PPF program implementers to better understand their experiences in designing and executing the program. Drawing on insights from these interviews, we have identified recommendations for future iterations of the PPF or similar programs.

Continue Providing a High Level of Coaching for Fellows

The program implementers flagged the mentorship program as one of the most successful aspects of the PPF program, stating that

> [t]he mentoring aspect of the fellowship is a successful innovation too. Fellows directly learned under the leadership of some of the best peace advocates and development workers in Mindanao. This allowed them to expand their networks, improve their direction in implementing projects, and gain lifelong mentors that can help them further their advocacies.

However, although most appreciated the mentorship program, several fellows experienced difficulty scheduling or attending meetings with their mentors over the course of the fellowship. Program implementers did consider geography when pairing fellows with mentors, but some fellows reported that it was difficult to physically connect with their mentor because they lived too far away and did not have the time and money to get to their mentor's office. In other cases, the fellows found that their mentors—often government leaders or attorneys—were simply too busy to meet with them.

Fellows spoke more highly of the coaching provided by the EAI program implementers. Fellows stated that the program implementers had been extraordinarily helpful in filling in for their assigned mentors, providing guidance whenever requested. According to the PPF fellows, the PPF staff constantly checked in on their progress and provided guidance, motivation, and support when needed. Although some fellows said that it was difficult to meet all of the demands of their fellowships, most felt that they had benefited from the required project reporting, webinars, volunteering, and mentoring. Some of the fellows also noted that PPF staff had helped them figure out how to maximize their seed funds to create the biggest effect. Ensuring that there are enough staff to continue and improve this level of support will be critical.

In addition to formal mentorship, the fellows drew on support from each other; for instance, two of the fellows established a "volunteer hub" for young professionals to help each other with their respective advocacy initiatives. The PPF Facebook group has served as a platform for the EAI staff to share resources and information with the fellows, although the fellows themselves primarily connect with each other in private messages or offline, rather than through the Facebook group.

Recognize and Address Fellows' Geographic and Connectivity Challenges

Although most fellows chose to implement projects in their own communities, two fellows decided to reach vulnerable populations in remote areas; in these cases, the fellows noted that the cost and difficulty of traveling to these areas presented challenges. More broadly, the geographic distribution of the fellows—who were located all across Mindanao—made it difficult for the program implementers to provide in-person support and monitoring. The program implementers noted that, although they made every effort to attend project-related events in person, they were simply unable to travel regularly to the locations of all the fellows, particularly those located in the far-flung island provinces.

Reliable internet and cell service was also an issue for several fellows. This affected the program implementers' ability to maintain consistent communications with all fellows and fellows' ability to remain connected with one another. Because of these connectivity issues, some fellows suggested that program implementers could help them promote their projects online. One interviewee elaborated on this issue, saying that "[w]e have problems with signal and electricity in our area, which sometimes causes delays in creating and posting content, especially if it has pictures or videos; so we really need help with more promotion and advertisement to further the reach of our projects."

Ultimately, program implementers need to recognize that fellows in distant locations and those who lack reliable internet connections do face special challenges. However, recruiting only fellows in central locations or fellows with stable internet connections would probably eliminate fellows who could work in conflict-prone areas that are in most critical need of an actively engaged civil society.

Program implementers said that the difficulties of monitoring and providing support to projects on a consistent, in-person basis was exacerbated by having a limited number of staff members, who all had professional responsibilities beyond the PPF program. Program implementers planned to hire a staff member specifically for the PPF program; the dedicated staff member could be available to travel to the locations of the various fellows to provide in-person support and monitoring.

Take Fellows' Time Constraints into Account When Designing Program Requirements

Fellows cited time constraints as one of their biggest obstacles to project implementation. Most fellows are full-time students or have full-time jobs. Nearly all of the fellows said that they had faced major issues with time management, often sacrificing personal or family time or their studies to work on their projects. As an interviewee with a full-time job explained, "Time is the biggest challenge. This project is not a full-time endeavor; I work full-time on top of it. Also, I cannot do this project alone so I have lots of volunteers, but they also have their own jobs and schedules, and convening them is hard." Another fellow, who is a full-time student, said that "[t]he major challenge is that I am still a student, so I find it difficult to manage time for studies and for this advocacy. At one point I noticed my performance in the classroom was slipping because I was spending too much time on my project." Some fellows requested that the program implementers be more conscious of their many commitments and allow more time to prepare reports and other assignments; one interviewee suggested turning the weekly report into a monthly report or cutting back on other requirements. Fellows did feel that the program implementers had been very understanding and flexible when asked for extensions on various assignments.

Program implementers said that they had made every effort to accommodate the schedules and other responsibilities of the fellows whenever an issue was brought to their attention, stating that "school and work always come first." The implementers also said that they had attempted to make it clear at the outset of the program how much of a time commitment these projects would require.

Program implementers suggested that selecting a few extra fellows at the start of the program might help offset the inevitable attrition. As stated earlier, most fellows enter the program with previous school or work responsibilities. Initially, 14 fellows participated in the PPF, but three did not complete their six-month fellowships. Two of the fellows underestimated the amount of time and dedication required to execute these projects; another fellow transferred to a new, more demanding job.

Consider Increasing Funding to Help Sustain Successful Projects

Several of the fellows stated that, although they were grateful for the seed funding they received, the limited amount of funding made it difficult to implement their projects or be too ambitious in their execution.[2] They also had trouble scaling up their projects and sustaining them beyond the six months of the fellowship. Fellows stated that they wanted to pursue and expand their projects (for instance, by expanding their model to different target audiences or other regions of Mindanao); fellows who had projects that were more limited in scope wanted to implement new peace projects. As part of the OURmindaNOW summit, fellows created one-to-three-year action plans, called sustainability maps, to scale up their projects (OURmindaNOW, undated); however, these plans would be difficult to implement without continued funding. As one interviewee put it, "[f]unding is number one: it's really hard to make progress on the project when most of the funding goes to transportation and food instead of being able to apply it to more activities." Another stated that "[w]e need more seed funds and planning to make our project more sustainable so that it won't just stop when the fellowship ends; I want to be able to make my project last in the future to keep helping my community."

Some fellows looked for outside donors during their projects, but they did not meet with much success. Others indicated that they

---

2 The fellows received 40,000 Philippine pesos (about $821); to put this amount in perspective, the average monthly salary after taxes in Davao City, Mindanao, is reportedly 12,833.33 Philippine pesos ($254.71) (see "Cost of Living in Davao," undated).

planned to partner with local government or with other organizations that share their mission. One of the program implementers noted that they sought to make the program more sustainable

> by attaching the fellows to existing local organizations [through the mentorship program] and increasing sustainability of those local organizations by giving them a new asset in the form of the fellow; this also ideally gives fellows the skills that can help lead them to new jobs [in the peace promotion space].

It remains to be seen whether this model will enable the fellows to continue their work. Some of the fellows already work in jobs related to development or peace promotion and they might be able to use their positions to help further their projects.

Help Fellows Develop Contingency Plans to Overcome Logistical Issues, Unforeseen Events

Some fellows mentioned facing unforeseen logistical issues while implementing their projects. Two fellows received pushback from the local government because their projects supposedly overlapped with government initiatives. A few interviewees noted that such circumstances as natural disasters and personal emergencies had disrupted or posed challenges to their projects. A series of earthquakes in Mindanao in fall 2019 and the eruption of Taal Volcano in January 2020 disrupted some projects. In addition, some fellows faced personal issues, such as health problems and family deaths; although they managed to adapt under these circumstances, they noted that they had not made contingency plans for such instances.

Finally, some fellows shared that their families were not supportive of their efforts, which created additional strife. According to one interviewee,

> [m]y family doesn't understand why I am doing this and they are often against it, telling me that I don't gain anything from this financially, mentally, or physically. But in spite of this, I am drawing on the guidance of the Almighty and the support of one of my

> grandparents and my best friend. If 1 million people say no and two say I can do it, I am determined to keep going.

Program implementers could emphasize developing contingency planning to help future PPF fellows avoid such logistical pitfalls.

In addition, a few fellows suggested that it would be helpful to provide step-by-step guides for project implementation; implementation information was provided through speakers at the PPF orientation, and fellows found it difficult to remember details when it came time to execute the project.

Help Peace Promotion Fellows Establish Social Networks

Some peace promotion fellows noted the difficulty of establishing networks to further the reach of their projects, with one interviewee saying "[i]n terms of scope, my project has not been as broad as expected; I thought I would be able to establish networks at different universities rather than just one, but that has proven tough to do." Another interviewee similarly stated, "I entered the peace promotion fellowship without a clear and solid network, so I entered the project implementation phase a bit blindly and didn't have an advocacy network to rely on."

Ensure That Fellows Have Credibility in Their Communities

One of the program implementers stated that the success of the PPF program hinges on the ability of the implementers to select fellows who have a credible voice in their communities and can effectively engage with at-risk youth. Fellows must come from communities where violent extremism is a palpable issue; if they are perceived as unrelatable, their message could go unheard. Therefore, it is important that tech camp and PPF fellows represent the whole spectrum of ideologies, locations, ethnic minorities, and geographically and socioeconomically marginalized groups. Program implementers seem to have accomplished this in the first iteration of the program, but it is an important element to bear in mind for future iterations.

CHAPTER FOUR

Conclusion

PPF fellows reported that the tech camp and the PPF program offered valuable experiences. They also offered several recommendations for improving the training. Fellows recommended that (1) the tech camp training include early introduction of the PPF program to allow participants to anticipate and apply for the PPF opportunity, (2) the curriculum load of the five-day PPF event be reduced so as not to overtax fellows, and (3) programming should include more break-out sessions to enable focused practice opportunities and more training on project management and implementation.

Overall, the fellowship component of the intervention appeared to generate a substantial amount of enthusiasm for CVE among the fellows. Fellows created a diverse array of initiatives, including awareness-raising campaigns about conflict and paths to peace in Mindanao, intercultural and interreligious exchanges, and educational initiatives meant to improve people's livelihoods. Fellows felt that their PPF projects had allowed them to make significant strides in their personal development as "influencers of peace" and had palpable effects on their respective communities.

Fellows mostly spoke positively of the support they received from EAI, noting that EAI mentorship and funding were critical in implementation of their programs. These fellows, together with EAI implementers, offered several recommendations for improving future efforts. These recommendations included recruiting more fellows to compensate for anticipated attrition; offering more funding to help build and sustain projects; helping fellows build social networks; offering logistical and contingency planning support; ensuring sufficient implementer staff to enable mentoring, oversight, and aid, especially for geographically dispersed fellows; and careful selection of fellows to ensure credibility.

Lessons for Future Evaluations

Few researchers have attempted to assess CVE-oriented tech camp trainings or CVE campaigns implemented by tech camp attendees. In this report, we present a qualitative assessment of EAI CVE programming in the Philippines, drawing primarily on the perspectives of the PPF program's key participants. This approach offers implementers and government funders insight into program implementation, helping identify ways in which programming can be improved.

A key limitation of our qualitative research is that participant appraisals might be biased in favor of the EAI implementers and represent an overly rosy picture of training and support. We also could not assess whether the training and fellowships improved participant use of social media or led to significant attitudinal or behavioral changes on the part of the intended audiences. Consequently, it will be critical for future training assessments to include more-quantitative assessments of process and effects.

We offer several recommendations for such quantitative assessments. First, evaluations should make better use of assessments of training quality. Training quality is subjective, but observational tools exist to help observers systematically assess whether training programs adhere to established best practices for training (Carroll et al., 2007; Weiss, Bloom, and Brock, 2014). We could not use these observational tools, but we strongly recommend that future studies take proper advantage of them.

Second, surveys conducted before and after the tech camp training can help determine whether the training met initial learning goals (Level 2 of Kirkpatrick's model). In Appendix B, we provide a specially tailored knowledge quiz to assess participant learning; a measure of social support, which can assess the degree to which participants feel supported by one another; and self-efficacy scales, which provide a valid and reliable way to measure perceived acquisition of skillsets.

Third, researchers and implementers could measure participant performance (Level 3 of Kirkpatrick's model) by collecting available data on participant social media. The ideal platform for measuring social media use is Twitter because collecting and analyzing Twitter posts and other such data are relatively easy. In contrast, Facebook privacy restrictions make it difficult to collect and analyze its data. Analysis of Twitter data, collected pre- and post-training, could reveal whether participants are posting more frequently (by averaging the number of tweets per month), posting more effectively (by averaging number of likes or retweets per tweet) and building a larger audience (by averaging number of followers). Analysis of Twitter data could also identify whether participants are tweeting more on CVE issues by using human or machine coding techniques to code the number of CVE themed posts (Sobhani, Mohammad, and Kiritchenko, 2016).

Finally, it would be ideal to assess the effects of the micro-CVE campaign on target audience attitudes and behavior (Level 4 of Kirkpatrick's model). This is the most challenging assessment, although several options are available. Studying the social networks of the PPF fellows might be effective; in theory, the influence of PPF fellows would reach their own social networks. Following those peer networks over time could document changes in pro-CVE relevant attitudes and behavior. It also might be possible to study the individuals who follow a fellow's Twitter account. Analysis of their respective Twitter accounts using newly developed lexical tools could document the effects of their Twitter activity (Marcellino et al., 2017).

APPENDIX A

Interview Instruments

RAND Philippines Peace Summit Interviews

Participant Number:

Consent

The RAND Corporation is partnering with Equal Access International to better understand your attitudes and perceptions about the tech camp training you participated in back in April or August. We also want to learn about how the training impacted your communication skills and understand your current efforts in countering violent extremism. RAND is a research organization that conducts research for national governments, foundations, and nonprofit organizations. You can learn more about RAND at www.rand.org.

To do this, we would like to speak with you for about 30 minutes, pending your availability. We will ask your opinions about the tech camp, your current media use, and about your current peace promotion project.

We will use information you provide to help EAI improve its programming. Our findings will be summarized in a research report.

Any assessments you provide of the tech camp training or EAI's support to you will be confidential and will not be associated in any way with your name or any other identifiable information.

For some participants we would like to highlight the individual CVE projects in our report. While we will not highlight your name or the name of other peace promotion fellows in our report we recognize that describing participant CVE projects may make it possible for readers to figure out who you are. We consequently want to give you the option of whether we describe your CVE project in our report. If you do choose to allow us to describe the CVE project and we choose to do so, then we will follow-back up with you and send you any relevant quotes from our report in advance of publication. You can retract permission at that time if you so wish. You can still participate in our interview now, even if you choose not to allow us to describe your project in our report.

The only potential risk you face by participating in our study is if we accidentally release information about you or identify you and your responses in any way. We will guard against this possibility in several ways. We will store your data in a password protected computer file. Instead of placing your name on surveys, we will use a unique ID number. The file that links your ID number and name will be stored in a separate file from your survey responses. After our study is completed, we will destroy any files with your name or other identifying information.

This study is voluntary. You are free to not answer any questions and you may stop participation at any time. Your decision to participate or not will have no impact on your relationship with RAND or EAI.

Your assistance and participation in this study is essential to the success of our research, so your time and cooperation is most appreciated.

If you have questions about this study, you can contact the research coordinator for this study at [redacted]. You can also contact RAND's Human Subject Protection Committee at [redacted].

Do you have any questions? Do you agree to participate in this interview? [yes/no answer]

Do you give us permission to describe your CVE project? [yes/no answer]

Interview Guide

Questions Related to the Tech Camp

1. What kind of things did you learn at the tech camp?

2. What did you like most about the tech camp?
3. What improvements would you suggest for the tech camp?
4. On a scale of 1–5, with 5 being excellent and 1 being poor, how would you rate the degree to which the tech camp prepared you for your current project? What else could the tech camp have taught you to prepare you for your current project?
5. Beyond your specific project, how else has the tech camp helped you?

Questions Related to the Peace Fellowship Projects

1. Can you tell me briefly about your current project or what you have been up to since the tech camp? How does your project counter or address violent extremism? What kinds of activities you are doing?
   a. Prompt (target audience): Who is the target audience for your program?
   b. Prompt (activities): What activities does your program engage in?
   c. Prompt (objectives): What are the goals or intended outcomes that you are trying to achieve with your program?
   d. Prompt (outputs): Can you tell me about any outputs? (number of people trained, number/frequency of social media posts, etc.)
   e. Prompt (outcome): What do you feel is the biggest impact your fellowship project has had on your community?
   f. Prompt (outcome): What do you expect to change as a result of the program?
   g. Prompt (evaluation): How do you know if your efforts were successful?
2. Why did you choose this project?
3. What are the biggest successes and challenges you have faced in implementing your project?
4. What type of ongoing support and mentorship are you receiving from EAI staff or from fellow participants?
5. What additional types of support would you like to have?

6. What could EAI and its partners do differently to better support you and other fellows in the future?
7. What do you plan to do next?
8. Final question, could we contact you again in one to two months to see how you and your project are doing at that time? [yes/no answer]

RAND Interviews with EAI Staff

Consent

Do you have any questions? Do you agree to participate in this interview? [yes/no answer]

Do you give us permission to quote you in our report? [yes/no answer]

Interview Guide

1. What types of training and support did you provide to PPF participants (in terms of funding, mentorship, networking, etc.)?
2. What were your goals and objectives for the PPF program?
3. In your opinion, what were the most successful aspects of the PPF program? Were there any specific PPF projects you view as being particularly successful?
4. What were the biggest challenges you encountered in supporting the PPF fellows?
5. What lessons did you learn regarding how to best implement the PPF program or similar programs in the future?

APPENDIX B

Tech Camp Assessment Instrument Results

We administered a survey instrument before and after training to the 30 participants attending EAI's first tech camp in April 2019. The surveys assess satisfaction ratings and changes in knowledge, self-confidence, and participant social support.

Tech camp training was intended to increase participant knowledge about key tactics and contextual information; participants would use this knowledge as part of a later micro-CVE campaign. In consultation with EAI, we created an 18-item true/false and multiple-choice instrument to assess whether participant knowledge improved. The instrument assessed knowledge on key topics, including CVE, Mindanao history, and social media use and tactics. Participants did experience a moderate, although statistically significant ($p < 0.05$) improvement in communication campaign knowledge as a result of the training (see Figure B.1).

We assumed that the five-day training event, held at a local hotel, would result in significant improvements in perceptions of social support. Participants would spend a full week together, both during the training and during the morning and evening hours, building relationships that they could use to improve the implementation of their campaigns. For example, support from a group of like-minded activists could improve individual motivation to engage in CVE activities, as well as the transfer of knowledge and skills. We used the "Friends" subscale of the Multidimensional Scale of Perceived Social Support (MSPSS), a frequently used measure, to assess social support. The full scale consists of 12 items (four questions are devoted to social support derived from

Figure B.1
Results of the Pretraining and Post-Training Knowledge Quizzes

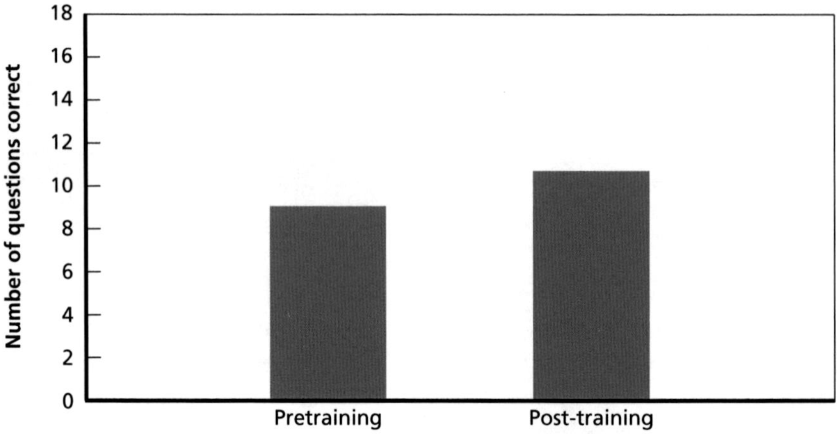

friends). Previous research has shown that this scale has high internal consistency and moderate construct validity (Zimet et al., 1988).[1]

Figure B.2 presents the results of our assessment of social support. Following training, participants evidenced a statistically significant increase in social support ($p < 0.001$).

We were unable to directly assess improvements in participant skills; however, we did create and administer a task-specific self-efficacy scale. Respondents were presented with a list of skills and asked to rate their degree of confidence on a scale of 0 ("cannot do at all") to ten ("highly certain can do"). Previous research has demonstrated the reliability and validity of self-efficacy scales, which have been adapted to address a variety of different task-specific behaviors and have been shown to correlate highly with actual performance (Dougherty, Johnston, and Thompson, 2007; Fouad, Smith, and Enochs, 1997; Gayton, Matthews, and Burchstead, 1986). The ten-item scale created for the EAI tech camp evaluated confidence in campaign design, telling stories, generat-

---

[1] We note that efforts to translate the MSPSS into foreign languages have not yielded as much success. According to Dambi et al. (2018), most translations were not rigorous and there was poor evidence for structural validity. The implications for this study are unclear because we administered the scale in English to an English-speaking audience.

Figure B.2
Results of the Pretraining and Post-Training Measures of Social Support

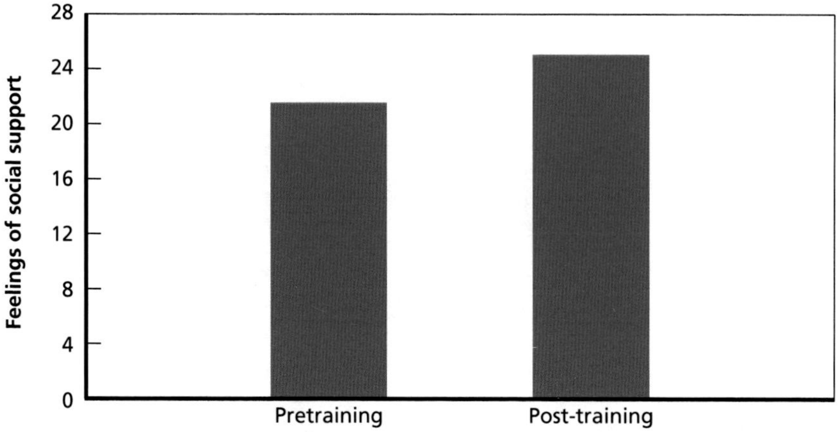

NOTE: Social support was measured through four items, each rated through a seven-point Likert scale (1 = "very strongly disagree" with the item; 7 = "very strongly agree" with the item). The highest score possible was 28 points.

ing social media, working with journalists, understanding CVE drivers, creating videos, public speaking, promoting peace and tolerance, using Facebook, and "bringing ideas to action."

As depicted in Figure B.3, the composite scale for all ten items shows significant improvement over baseline ($p < 0.001$). Analysis of individual scales suggested that participants experienced the most improvement in campaign design, telling stories, generating viral social media content, working with journalists, understanding CVE drivers, and knowing how to create interesting video content (see Figure B.4). We did not conduct statistical analyses on these comparisons. Effects were muted for the other individual scales.

Finally, we assessed participant satisfaction with the training. Figure B.5 presents the results of five satisfaction questions. Participants uniformly rated all aspects of the training highly.

In conclusion, tech camp training led to moderate but significant improvements in outcomes related to knowledge, social support, and self-efficacy. In addition, participants offered high ratings on a satisfaction scale.

Figure B.3
Results of the Ten-Item Composite Self-Efficacy Scale

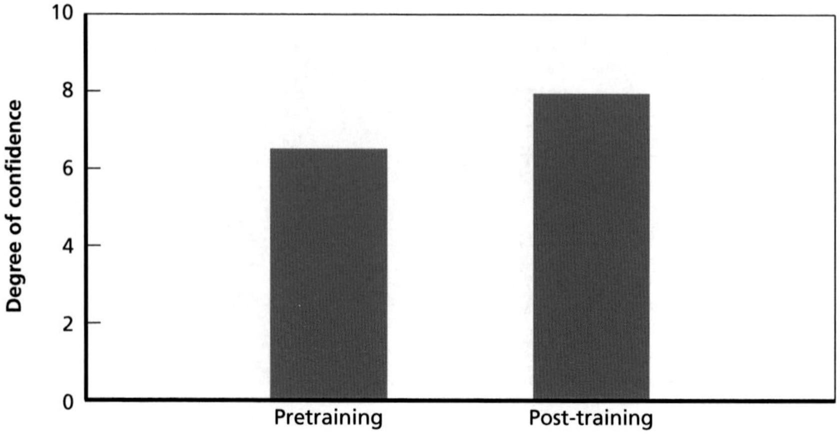

Figure B.4
The Six Self-Efficacy Scale Items That Showed the Most Improvement

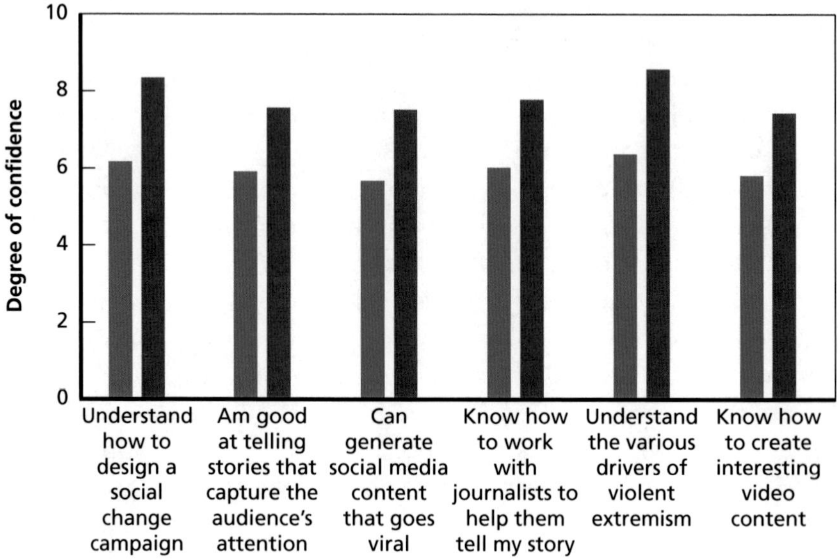

Figure B.5
Results of Five-Item Satisfaction Scale

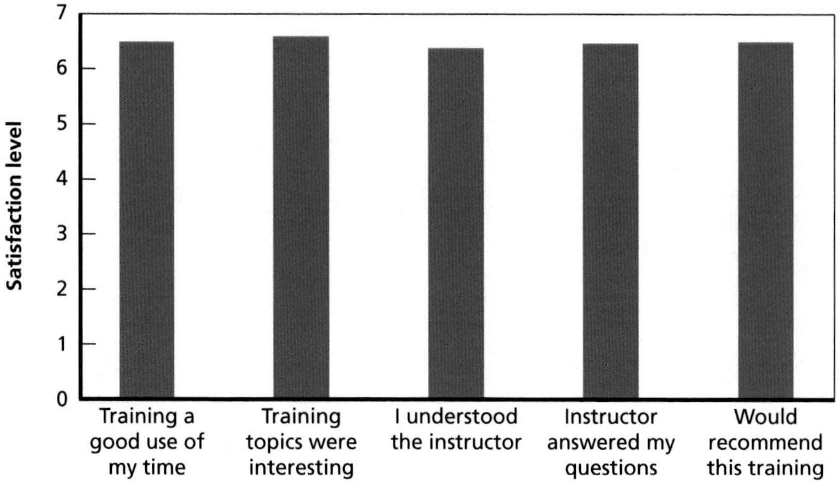

NOTE: Satisfaction was measured through a seven-point Likert scale (1 = "very strongly disagree"; 7 = "very strongly agree").

APPENDIX C

Summary of Peace Promotion Fellowship Projects

Table C.1 presents the 11 projects implemented by EAI PPF fellows, including their geographic areas of implementation, objectives, target audiences, activities, and outputs.

Table C.1
Summary of Peace Promotion Projects

Project Title	Geographic Area	Descriptions[a]	Objective	Target Audience	Activities	Reported Outputs[b]
Bangsamoro Youth Peacebuilding	Cotabato City, Maguindanao	"Bangsamoro Youth Peacebuilding aims to gather youth leaders representing orphanages, in-school youth community-based and church-based organizations, and indigenous people in Cotabato City and Maguindanao. This project fosters social cohesion as a method of [PTVE]."	"The project [aims] to capacitate and empower youth leaders to become frontline peace influencers among their peers and the community."	Youth leaders from various community organizations	• Team-building exercises for volunteers • Volunteering at orphanages and retirement homes	• Trained 20 youth leaders • Convened 12 youth mentors • Served 220 orphans and 29 residents in the home of the abandoned and sick • Recruited 29 volunteers • Conducted three workshops, two community immersions, and one team-building exercise • Reached approximately 46,700 people online, with 20 people posting regularly • Created six training modules

Table C.1—Continued

Project Title	Geographic Area	Descriptions[a]	Objective	Target Audience	Activities	Reported Outputs[b]
PEACEsonality	Cotabato City, Maguindanao	"PEACEsonality is a peacebuilding and capacity development project focused on personality development, peace promotion, and PTVE."	"The project aims to develop a positive mental attitude among at-risk youth as it creates a peaceful and resilient society."	Out-of-school youth, orphans, youth in conflict-affected areas, and youth prone to suicidal depression	• Training on social media use for storytelling and messaging purposes • Public speaking workshop	• Trained eight facilitators • Reached about 1,000 people online • Recruited 15 youth participants in program
In The Loop	Davao City, Davao del Sur	"In The Loop Initiative is a youth-centered, culturally sensitive, and artistic approach to peace advocacy that will tackle prevention and transformation of violent extremism, tri-people representation, and peace education starting with a pilot program called the Peace Education Symposium."	"This project will tap [into] the strong culture and arts scene of Davao to release stickers, narratives, short stories, poems, and other art forms to instigate and normalize conversations about peace."	University and high school students	• Art workshops • Writing poetry on topics related to violent extremism • Cultural tours	• Reached about 900 people through Facebook posts • Received 200 page likes on Facebook • Recruited ten actively engaged volunteers

Table C.1—Continued

Project Title	Geographic Area	Descriptions[a]	Objective	Target Audience	Activities	Reported Outputs[b]
Community of Peace (*BansaKulToura*)	Bongao, Tawi-Tawi	"Community of Peace is an online and offline youth dialogue platform that promotes the understanding of peace through faith and lifestyle similarities."	"The project aspires to [provide] vulnerable youth from [Tawi-Tawi] [with] an alternative [way to spend] their idle time to avoid the allure of [violent extremist organization] recruitment."	Youth, especially elementary and high school students	• Education activities for children • Training workshops for teachers on specific peace-related topics	• Conducted four cultural events • Engaged 239 children and 25 teachers or administrators through events • Some Facebook posts reached up to 60,000 people online
Project ComMUnity	Kabuntalan, Maguindano	"Project ComMUnity [takes] an interfaith approach [to] building the capacities of community and local government members to improve their participation and initiatives in providing solutions to violent extremism and other security issues in their *barangay*."	"The project [seeks to] strengthen the collaboration of the community and local government as equal peace actors."	*Barangay* leaders, women, youth, and other members of the community	• Leadership management workshop with *barangay* leaders and youth • Conflict resolution workshop	• Trained 42 members of the community to help implement project • Reached up to 2,300 people online

Table C.1—Continued

Project Title	Geographic Area	Descriptions[a]	Objective	Target Audience	Activities	Reported Outputs[b]
Balik Lantaw	Tagoloan, Misamis Oriental	"*Balik Lantaw* tackles the tri-people and conflict history of Mindanao through a peer-to-peer approach among students and capacitates them as young peace influencers."	The project "aims to raise the awareness of selected in-school youth about cultural sensitivity, the tri-people of the island, and the ethno-history of Mindanao [to provide a] potential alternative narrative through peer-to-peer education. This project [also] intends to partner with local government in institutionalizing a peer education module on peacebuilding and transforming violent extremism."	Students in the four national high schools	• "Train the trainers" workshops for youth leaders • "Peace camp" involving poster making, extemporaneous speaking, and essay writing	• Trained four student body presidents of the four national schools; three youth leaders; and two Bangsamoro youth • Reached about 3,000 people through posts, primarily on Facebook

Table C.1—Continued

Project Title	Geographic Area	Descriptions[a]	Objective	Target Audience	Activities	Reported Outputs[b]
Pagmata ("Wake Up")	Del Carmen, Siargao, Surigao del Norte	"*Pagmata* is a [weekly] participatory radio program" that "discusses the importance of the family in promoting and building peace in the community."	The project "aims to raise awareness about peace-related issues in the community, provide the community [with a forum to voice] their questions and concerns, and inspire inclusion in the decision-making process in proposing potential solutions to the threats of [violent extremist organization] recruitment."	Parents and children in the community	• Radio show on CVE-related topics • Family peace day event	• Reached 5,425 listeners in three towns and 24 *barangays* • Held one family peace day event with 83 attendees • Reached about 5,770 people through posts on Facebook

Table C.1—Continued

Project Title	Geographic Area	Descriptions[a]	Objective	Target Audience	Activities	Reported Outputs[b]
Pag Iskul Ha	Patikul, Sulu	"*Pag Iskul Ha* initiates peace educational activities for internally displaced children who are in tent-based evacuation centers."	"*Pag Iskul Ha* focuses on providing safe spaces for children to learn peace education and resist violence by expressing themselves and becoming resilient. It will use a reading enhancement manual that has topics on values and forgiveness and at the same time enhances [the children's] skills in the English language."	Internally displaced children ages eight through 12	• Lectures on topics related to CVE • Literacy campaign • Learning activities for children (e.g., drawing, coloring, reading aloud) • Training workshops for teachers on specific peace-related topics • Building bridges in previously inaccessible regions	• 19 lectures • One luncheon with guest speaker on topic of peace and Islam • Posts on Facebook reached up to 1,000 people
SUSTAINable YOUth (Project *Edukasyon* 2030)	Silangkum, Tipo-Tipo	"SUSTAINable YOUth is a youth project using the Global Citizenship" pedagogical method "that adopts a lifelong learning approach in promoting sustainable development [that] contributes to an inclusive and peaceful society."	"The project aims to give a global perspective, promote sustainable livelihood programs, and produce a series of activities intended to build community resilience."	Students, out-of-school youth, teachers, parents, and various community stakeholders	• Education activities for children • Training workshops for teachers on specific peace-related topics • Educational camp on sustainable development goals	• Reached over 1,000 people on Facebook • Trained 23 teachers

Table C.1—Continued

Project Title	Geographic Area	Descriptions[a]	Objective	Target Audience	Activities	Reported Outputs[b]
Teen Trail for Peace	Cagayan de Oro, Misamis Oriental	"Teen Trail for Peace implements inter-faith and inter-cultural exchange awareness campaigns to [promote] cultural sensitivity toward others through workshops, [dialogue], and forums."	The project "aims to promote cultural sensitivity [among] college students with different cultural backgrounds, develop new skills in relaying the positive message of cultural sensitivity, and involve university student government in creating resolutions on cultural stigmatization in schools as a precautionary measure that supports the prevention of [violent extremist organization] recruitment in universities."	High school and university students	• Training on social media use for story-telling and messag-ing purposes • Intercultural exchanges	• Received 465 likes on Facebook within three months of starting page • Reached about 3,000 people online through Facebook posts • Convened 25 uni-versity leaders for first intercultural exchange; convened 13 high school stu-dents for second event

Table C.1—Continued

Project Title	Geographic Area	Descriptions[a]	Objective	Target Audience	Activities	Reported Outputs[b]
BukidKnown	Kalilangan, Bukidnon	"*BukidKnown* is an awareness campaign and intercultural exchange program that fosters understanding of co-existence and social cohesion as a method in preventing and transforming violent extremism."	The project "aims to reach out to the Talaandig communities in Bukidnon, particularly in Barangay Kalubnganan, highlighting the concept of meaningful travel among vloggers, community immersion, rights education, and empowering cultural communities."	Youth in various communities	• Intercultural exchanges • Cultural performances • Environmental activities, such as planting trees • Efforts to develop tourism industry in indigenous communities (e.g., training tour guides)	• Engaged with over 90 households (about 500 people) in indigenous communities • Reached about 46,000 people online through Facebook posts

[a] Descriptions are taken from OURmindaNOW, undated, and EAI, undated b.
[b] These outputs are taken from interviews with PPF fellows and are current as of February 1, 2020.

APPENDIX D

Results of a Study of Countering Violent Extremism–Themed Radio Programming in Mindanao

We have conducted successful randomized controlled trials of CVE-themed media programming in Nigeria and Indonesia. In Nigeria, we conducted a randomized encouragement design to test the effects of a CVE-themed radio talk show called *Ina Mafita* (Marrone et al., 2020). We recruited 2,064 participants in northern Nigeria via text messaging and assigned them to listen to either *Ina Mafita* or a control program (professional soccer matches) each week over the course of two months. We monitored compliance by texting participants a weekly quiz question that tested whether they had listened to their assigned program. Correct answers to the quiz earned a small financial incentive. Baseline and monthly surveys were also delivered via text message. Our results indicate that *Ina Mafita* had a positive effect on listeners' beliefs about the importance of being a role model and a positive—but not significant—effect on belief in local committees' value in reintegrating at-risk youth. Results were more pronounced for the high complier subsample and for those who reported liking the show's storyline.

In Indonesia, we recruited over 900 Indonesian youth via Facebook and randomly assigned them to systematically observe either CVE-themed Facebook posts or control content each week over the course of two months (Bodine-Baron et al., 2020). Surveys were conducted through an online portal. The results indicated that audiences recognized and liked the CVE-themed content at levels comparable with content derived from popular Indonesian advertisement and public service announcement campaigns. Results showed positive treatment effects at the end of the survey period regarding attitudes toward promoting inclusivity online, although the effect was the result of an unusual and sudden drop in attitudes of the participants in the control group. In addition, the effect was not robust to alternative regression specifications. There also were strong, significant negative treatment effects regarding respondents' attitudes toward living in separated communities.

Overall, both panel studies were conducted successfully. We recruited a large sample of participants through nontraditional methods of data collection (text message and Facebook advertisements) and were able to retain a significant share of the participants for the duration of the surveys.[1] Both studies demonstrated that small financial incentives motivated participants to listen to or view the CVE content on a routine basis.[2] (In the case of the Nigerian study, the incentive was supplemented by text messages that offered the participants reminders to listen to the assigned program.)

Drawing on the success of these studies, we conducted follow-on panel research in the Philippines. We recruited 1,200 participants in Mindanao and randomly assigned them to listen to either a locally broadcast CVE radio program or to a control condition. The research was initiated only five months after the Bangsomoro Autonomous Region in Muslim Mindanao (BARMM) was established on March 29, 2019. The BARMM allows for an autonomous government in select regions of Muslim Mindanao. Without question, the period of performance for this research was a time of significant change.[3]

---

1 For the Nigerian study, more than 90 percent of the sample responded to survey requests in the first 15 weeks of the study. At Week 32, the response rates dropped to 88 percent for the treatment group and 83 percent for the control group (Marrone et al., 2020). In the Indonesian study, the rate of response to survey requests at weeks 5, 10, and 15 ranged from 76 to 89 percent (Bodine-Baron et al., 2020).

2 In Nigeria, participants could earn the equivalent of $1 for every quiz question they answered correctly. In Indonesia, participants were paid the equivalent of $1.22 for taking a brief survey that included the treatment or control social media content.

3 Our operating theory was that a well-conducted communication campaign that helped in part to educate audiences of the benefits and success of the BARMM could improve attitudes toward the BARMM and improve citizen participation.

The treatment intervention in question was a radio drama called *Saranggola*. The show, which was produced by EAI, follows the story of Omar and his childhood friend Akmad, who both hail from a Muslim community in Mindanao. Akmad is now part of a rebel group, called Al Sinaan, and his journey into and, ultimately, out of this organization is one of several key storylines in the broadcast. Through Omar, Akmad, and the characters Hadja Patima and Radiya, the 48-episode broadcast seeks to promote, in three consecutive themes, youth empowerment, women's empowerment, and support of and participation in good governance (Calungsod, 2019). Our research was timed to assess the latter two of these themes: women's empowerment and support of and participation in good governance.

Ultimately, our research did not meet the same success as our initiatives in Nigeria and Indonesia. Treatment and control groups were not equivalent on key demographic variables, a series of earthquakes that shook Mindanao during the survey's initial weeks affected several data integrity measures, and analyses of attitudinal and knowledge outcomes showed a highly unusual pattern of results. These challenges lessened our confidence in the study results.

Consequently, in lieu of a formal publication, we wish to use this appendix to summarize the challenges that we encountered and offer lessons learned for future evaluations. First, we provide a brief summary of the research design. Next, we review three key challenges confronted in the execution phase. Finally, we offer lessons learned from this experience.

Approach

We contracted Kadence International, a Manila-based survey research firm, to conduct this research. To design the survey instrument for this evaluation, we worked closely with EAI to understand the operating theory of change and logic model. EAI staff identified the key goals of the radio program; we then developed survey questions designed to address these intended knowledge, attitude, and behavioral goals. We then worked with Kadence International to pilot test the survey questions in Davao City with a small sample of individuals recruited for this purpose. We made final revisions to the planned survey questions based on participant feedback. Our final questions are presented in Table D.1.

Figure D.1 presents a schematic of the study design. We recruited participants in preselected *barangays* in the provinces of Cotabato, Cotabato City, Lanao del Norte, and Maguindanao. We assigned participants at the *barangay* level to one of two conditions: the *Saranggola* radio show or locally aired basketball matches. We used this cluster assignment approach to account for possible spillover effects for each show caused by communication between participants within a community. The number of recruited participants per *barangay* ranged from 22 to 44 (mean: 24, median: 22). Before beginning the selection process, staff from Kadence International ensured that each *barangay* had transmission access to the *Saranggola* broadcast. Before the study began, RAND staff traveled to and observed survey staff training in Davao City.[4]

Survey staff were assigned to a particular *barangay* for baseline recruitment. They were asked to conduct a random sampling strategy that would begin at the *barangay* town hall, a health center, a school, or a church.[5] Survey participants needed to be within the 18-to-40 age

---

4 In Lanao del Norte, a more secure area, survey teams were composed of ten field interviewers and one area leader, with one interviewer assigned to one *barangay*. In each of the remaining areas, there were nine field interviewers and one area leader, and all interviewers surveyed a single *barangay* at a time. Efforts were made to ensure that individual interviewers were assigned to separate neighborhoods, with interviewers approaching houses alone. The survey teams (excepting in Lanao del Norte) were also accompanied by *barangay* officials because of security concerns and a mandate by the *barangays*. The *barangay* officials did not participate in interviews, although participants may have seen them. We did not know that these officials were involved in the surveys until after they were completed. Area leaders observed fieldwork and conducted follow-up phone calls during all phases of the surveys. At least 10 percent of the interviews were directly observed; 20 percent of the remaining interviews received follow-up phone calls.

5 In urban *barangays*, survey staff were instructed to visit every sixth house encountered on their walk assignment; in rural *barangays*, they were told to visit every third house.

Table D.1
Outcome Questions

Number	Label	Question	Answer Scale
1	Knowledge 1	Which of the following individuals is a former congressperson and a peace promoter?	Multiple choice
2	Knowledge 2	As part of the Bangsomoro Organic Law (BOL), residents will be able to elect their own parliament.	True; false; don't know
3	Knowledge 3	Compared with the [Autonomous Region in Muslim Mindanao], the BARMM will not have more control over how it spends money.	True; false; don't know
4	Women's Empowerment 1	"Women, just as well as men, can help improve society."	5-point scale (1 = strongly agree, 5 = strongly disagree)
5	Women's Empowerment 2	"A woman would not make an ideal candidate for political office."	5-point scale (1 = strongly agree, 5 = strongly disagree)
6	Women's Empowerment 3	In the past two months, to what extent have you encouraged a female friend or family member to get involved in their community (e.g., performing community work, promoting peace, attending meetings, helping local residents, running for office)?	3-point scale (1 = never, 2 = encouraged at least one person, 3 = encouraged more than one person)
7	Government Satisfaction 1a	To what extent are you satisfied with the progress of the BARMM? [only if in BARMM]	5-point scale (1 = very satisfied, 5 = very dissatisfied) with option "I am unfamiliar with the BARMM"
8	Government Satisfaction 1b	To what extent are you satisfied with the progress of the provincial government? [only if outside BARMM]	5-point scale (1 = very satisfied, 5 = very dissatisfied)

Table D.1—Continued

Number	Label	Question	Answer Scale
9	Government Satisfaction 2	To what extent are you satisfied with the national government?	5-point scale (1 = very satisfied, 5 = very dissatisfied)
10	Political Engagement 1	"People like me can make their community a better place to live."	5-point scale (1 = strongly agree, 5 =strongly disagree)
11	Political Engagement 2	"It is important that people like me regularly attend community assemblies or other community meetings held by the local government."	5-point scale (1 = strongly agree, 5 = strongly disagree)
12	Political Engagement 3	In the past two months, to what extent have you attended a community assembly or other local government meeting?	3-point scale (1 = never, 2 = one meeting, 3 = more than one meeting)
13	Religious Diversity	"Religious diversity in Mindanao is a good thing."	5-point scale (1 = strongly agree, 5 = strongly disagree)

Figure D.1
Randomized Trial Survey Design

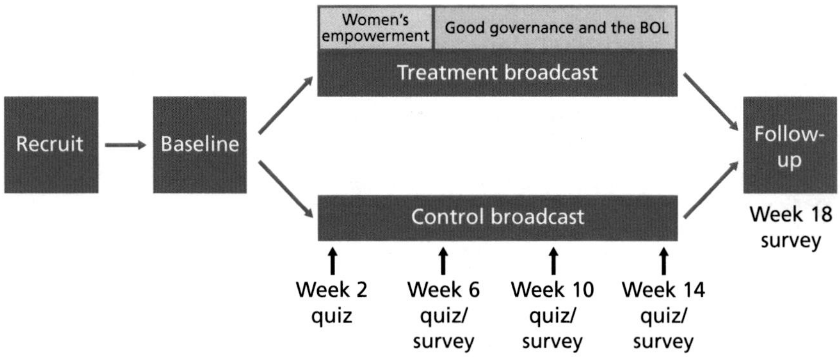

range, have proven access to AM radio at home,[6] speak and understand Tagalog (the language of *Saranggola*), and have no plans for travel during the next six months. After they consented to the survey, participants were provided instructions on listening to their assigned program and were administered the baseline survey.[7] For each of the next 14 weeks, participants received text-message reminders to listen to their assigned program. Treatment group participants were also reminded of the program's time and radio frequency.

Surveyors conducted follow-up waves at weeks 2, 6, 10, 14, and 18 after recruitment. In each of the first four follow-up waves, participants were asked a random set of two to four quiz questions about either the plot of *Saranggola* or the outcome of the basketball games. Participants earned 25 Philippine pesos (50 cents) for each correct answer. Weeks 6, 14, and 18 corresponded to the conclusion of each *Saranggola* storyline and a one-month follow-up. During these waves, participants were again asked the set of outcome questions listed in Table D.1. They were

---

6 Survey staff asked each participant to demonstrate that they could access the radio station that was scheduled to air *Saranggola* or the basketball game in that particular *barangay*.

7 Participants were supposed to agree to participate, then receive their assignment to the control or treatment group. However, Kadence International revised this portion of the procedure without informing our staff and told participants which group they would enter before securing their agreement (for more information, see the "Key Challenges" section).

then paid the equivalent of 102 Philippine pesos ($2) for participation, in addition to whatever they earned on quiz questions. If participants answered each quiz question right and participated in each survey, they could earn a total of 844 Philippine pesos ($16.50) for completing all surveys.

Key Challenges

Gender Difference Between Groups Revealed Selection Bias

The baseline survey showed a large gender imbalance between treatment and control groups: Thirty-one percent of the treatment group were men, compared with 66 percent of the control group. Kadence International field staff revealed that they had changed the study consent procedures so that participants were told in advance of their assigned group. (Kadence International staff made this change, without our knowledge, after the surveyor training event attended by RAND staff.) Women, out of a lack of interest or because of the cultural unacceptability of listening to basketball games, declined participation in the control group at disproportionate rates; men declined participation in the treatment group at disproportionate rates.

This change in consent procedure creates a self-selection problem that compromises the validity of the randomization and creates significant problems for making direct comparisons between the treatment and control group. We decided to conduct separate analyses for each group. Although this is not ideal, we reasoned that the sample was sufficiently large to detect significant differences from baseline to follow-up measures.

Natural Disasters Occurred During Data Collection

A series of severe earthquakes struck Mindanao within a month of subject recruitment. A 6.3-magnitude quake struck Mindanao on October 16, 2019, approximately one week before the scheduled week 2 quiz surveys. This was followed by a 6.6-magnitude earthquake on October 29, and a 6.5-magnitude aftershock on October 31. These two earthquakes, which were centered in Cotabato Province, reportedly killed

14 and injured 403 (Hollingsworth, 2019). Additional aftershocks occurred in the following two weeks (Save the Children, undated). Finally, a 5.9-magnitude earthquake struck Mindanao on November 18 ("Magnitude 5.9 Quake Shakes Bukidnon, Part of Mindanao," 2019). This later quake caused a two-week delay in data collection, which was supposed to begin on November 16.

We discovered a marked drop in participants' ability to correctly answer quiz questions. Specifically, the treatment group's quiz accuracy rate was 41 percent during week 6, compared with a 78-percent accuracy rate during week 2 and a 76-percent accuracy rate during week 10. The control group had a smaller drop in accuracy rate; generally, their accuracy rate was more than 80 percent, but it fell to 61 percent during week 6. This fall might have been caused by an inability to access programming; when a random subset of participants was phoned to conduct routine data checks, 61 percent reported a weak or choppy signal on the *Saranggola* radio station in the wake of the earthquakes. Disruptions in daily life also could have contributed to a reduction in radio listenership.

Analyses of data quality indicators show weak quality for week 6. Pairwise correlations in responses to particular questions show weaker correlation in week 6 than in other weeks. Furthermore, Cronbach's alpha, a coefficient of reliability, shows weaker reliability for week 6. Typically, the more a group of questions measure the same underlying construct, the higher Cronbach's alpha is (on a scale from 0 to 1). An alpha value of 0.70 or above is generally considered sufficient. For some (but not all) outcome questions, responses in week 6 show very poor reliability compared with other weeks. For example, comparing responses regarding satisfaction with the BARMM, responses in week 6 have an alpha coefficient of just 0.01, compared with between 0.5 and 0.6 in other weeks.

Given problems in data quality for week 6, we have decided to not analyze that wave of data and instead focus on weeks 14 and 18. However, none of the reliability coefficients for any question exceeded 0.70, which reinforces our belief that the outcomes may be measuring something other than effects of *Saranggola*, as explained in more detail in the following section.

Control and Treatment Groups Show Strikingly Similar Results

Analysis of treatment group data shows highly significant results, which is unusual for communications campaigns, such as *Saranggola*. Treatment participants reported some positive effects: They were better satisfied with government and had more-positive perceptions of women's ability to participate in civic and governmental life. There was also evidence of negative effects: Treatment participants also felt less engaged in participation in government decisionmaking and were less accepting of religious diversity.

However, the control group had nearly the exact same trends in response as the treatment group. Even for noisy outcomes (in which the follow-up measure varied between positive and negative over time), the control group patterns matched the treatment group. Noisy outcomes are not unusual for opinion surveys, but the strong correlation in response between treatment and control groups is highly unusual.

Figures D.2 and D.3 show the changes from baseline for treatment and control groups in three outcome indexes constructed from the questions in Table D.1.[8] The dotted line indicates results from week 6, which we discount. For weeks 14 and 18, some outcomes are very large. Regarding the questions about women's empowerment, the treatment group in Week 18 shows a 0.46 standard deviation increase in agreement with the sentiments of *Saranggola* relative to baseline. This effect size is enormous for a communications campaign and raises questions on its own. In addition, this enormous effect was also seen in the control group, which was only exposed to basketball games.

These large swings in outcome with near-perfect correlation in both groups is further evidence of possible data quality problems. We analyzed data quality and interviewed Kadence International personnel to determine whether these patterns were introduced by errors in

[8] For the regression, opinions in each week were standardized against the baseline distribution to form a *z*-score. Indexes were formed as equally weighted averages of these normalized scores. The regression coefficients can then be interpreted as the number of standard deviations by which the average opinion index changed. For other questions, outcomes were turned into binary variables, with indexes calculated as equally weighted averages. The regression coefficient for the knowledge index is then interpreted as the change in the fraction of correct answers.

Figure D.2
Treatment Group Changes in Opinions

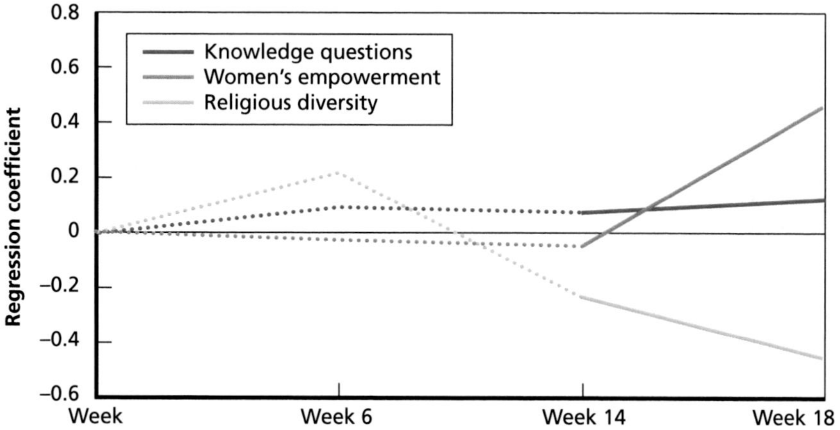

NOTES: This figure depicts regression coefficients for survey wave dummies in regression of outcome indexes on survey wave and individual characteristics. Positive numbers indicate correct answers for the knowledge questions and positive sentiment for the women's empowerment and religious diversity questions; negative numbers indicate incorrect answers for the knowledge questions and negative sentiment for the women's empowerment and religious diversity questions. Indexes were constructed as averages of thematically grouped outcome questions (as shown in Table D.1). Regressions were clustered at the *barangay* level. All outcomes in weeks 14 and 18 are statistically significant at the 5-percent level.

the survey software or via systematic manipulation of responses by survey personnel. We found no evidence for these explanations.

One explanation for these significant shifts in opinion is that outside events unrelated to study participation affected participants' views. This might explain why both groups showed parallel, sustained improvements in our three main knowledge outcomes, including understanding of the terms of the BOL. Media coverage of events involving the new BARMM might have improved participants' knowledge, which could have driven changes in the attitudes measured in this study. This coverage might have been much stronger and more strongly received than a newly established radio show.

Kadence International documented several BARMM- and BOL-related events that made regional or national headlines during the

Figure D.3
Control Group Changes in Opinions

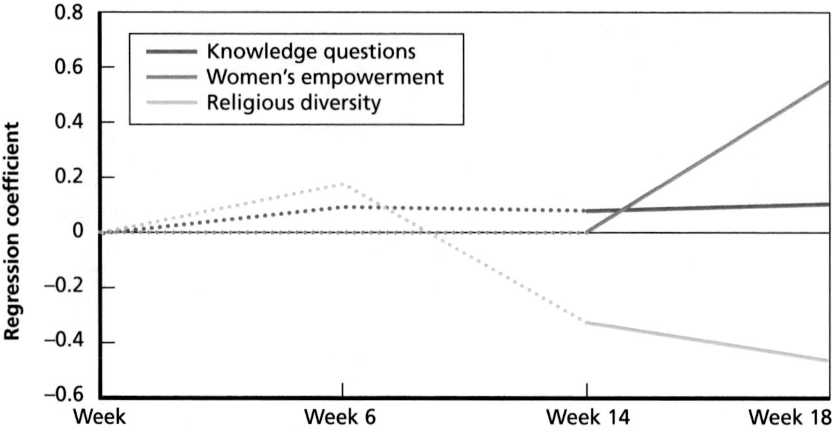

NOTES: This figure depicts regression coefficients for survey wave dummies in regression of outcome indexes on survey wave and individual characteristics. Positive numbers indicate correct answers for the knowledge questions and positive sentiment for the women's empowerment and religious diversity questions; negative numbers indicate incorrect answers for the knowledge questions and negative sentiment for the women's empowerment and religious diversity questions. Indexes were constructed as averages of thematically grouped outcome questions (as shown in Table D.1). Regressions were clustered at the *barangay* level. All outcomes in weeks 14 and 18 are statistically significant at the 5-percent level.

course of the survey. These events could have raised substantive awareness of the BOL.

Conclusions

What can be done to mitigate or avoid these challenges in future research? Greater oversight of data collection may be warranted. Better oversight of participant recruitment might have prevented Kadence International from making the changes in the consent form that led to this research's self-selection issues. Our staff did not shadow survey personnel during recruitment because it was felt that our presence might influence participants' agreement to participate or their responses to the baseline survey.

BARMM- and BOL-Related News Headlines from Mindanao During the Study Period

November 13, 2019: "BARMM Cabinet Reshuffled: Ebrahim to Serve as Finance Minister"

Ahod Ebrahim, interim chief minister of BARMM and Moro Islamic Liberation Front chairman, also took on the position of BARMM finance minister (Arguillas, 2019a).

November 21, 2019: "NorthCot Turns Over 63 Barangays to Bangsamoro Region"

The 63 *barangays* in North Cotabato that voted yes to BARMM inclusion in February 2019 were formally turned over on this day. Several areas covered in our study were included in this turnover (Cabrera, 2019).

December 1, 2019: "PhP 65.6-B Budget for Bangsamoro 2020 Approved; Education Gets Biggest Chunk"

This was the first time that the BARMM appropriated its own funds (Arguillas, 2019b).

January 30, 2020: "Senate Asks BTA to Name Reps to Congress—Bangsamoro Parliament Forum"

Juan Miguel Zubiri, the Senate majority leader, was working with Bangsamoro Transition Authority leaders to determine the future Bangsamoro Transition Authority representatives in the Philippine Congress (Arguillas, 2020a).

February 17, 2020: "Cotabato City Seeks Exclusion from BARMM Until June 30, 2022"

The mayor of Cotabato City called for the city to be excluded from the BARMM until the election on June 30, 2020, stating that the BARMM was not yet "fully functioning" (Arguillas, 2020b).

In addition, Mindanao is a relatively isolated island, with varied geographical terrain; several religions, ethnicities, and languages; limited infrastructure; dangerous security conditions; and an evolving political environment. Our research required surveyors to recruit 1,200 participants and engage in repeated survey visits and quizzes over the course of 20 weeks. We are not aware of any other study undertaken on Mindanao with such an ambitious research plan, but perhaps this plan was too ambitious.

Given an opportunity to repeat this evaluation, we likely would attempt a simpler method of research, such as focus group testing. We originally avoided focus group testing because EAI had planned its own focus group–style testing, and we wanted to avoid replication. We had planned to conduct focus groups following the household survey to complement (rather than substitute for) the quantitative results, but the groups were cancelled because of the dangers posed by COVID-2019.

Focus groups could have provided insight into the effectiveness of the program, if not a full evaluation of its effects. Focus group-participants would have been exposed to one or two broadcasted episodes. We then could have collected information on the likeability of the program, the perceived intent of the program, and the ways that the program challenged audience members. These results could have been useful to both the sponsor of the program and the broader academic community.

References

Ackerman, Spencer, "Newest U.S. Counterterrorism Strategy: Trolling," *Wired*, July 18, 2012. As of August 11, 2020:
https://www.wired.com/2012/07/counterterrorism-trolls

Arguillas, Carolyn O., "BARMM Cabinet Reshuffled: Ebrahim to Serve as Finance Minister," *Mindanews*, November 13, 2019a. As of August 17, 2020:
https://www.mindanews.com/peace-process/2019/11/
barmm-cabinet-reshuffled-ebrahim-to-serve-as-finance-minister

———, "PhP 65.6-B Budget for Bangsamoro 2020 Approved; Education Gets Biggest Chunk," *Mindanews*, December 1, 2019b. As of August 17, 2020:
https://www.mindanews.com/peace-process/2019/12/
php-65-6-b-budget-for-bangsamoro-2020-approved-education-gets-biggest-chunk

———, "Senate Asks BTA to Name Reps to Congress—Bangsamoro Parliament Forum," *Mindanews*, January 30, 2020a. As of August 17, 2020:
https://www.mindanews.com/peace-process/2020/01/
senate-asks-bta-to-name-reps-to-congress-bangsamoro-parliament-forum

———, "Cotabato City Seeks Exclusion from BARMM Until June 30, 2022," *Mindanews*, February 17, 2020b. As of August 17, 2020:
https://www.mindanews.com/peace-process/2020/02/
cotabato-city-seeks-exclusion-from-barmm-until-june-30-2022

Bodine-Baron, Elizabeth, James V. Marrone, Todd C. Helmus, and Danielle Schlang, *Countering Violent Extremism in Indonesia: Using an Online Panel Survey to Assess a Social Media Counter-Messaging Campaign*, Santa Monica, Calif.: RAND Corporation, RR-A233-1, 2020. As of August 17, 2020:
https://www.rand.org/pubs/research_reports/RRA233-1

Cabrera, Ferdinandh B., "NorthCot Turns Over 63 Barangays to Bangsamoro Region," *Mindanews*, November 21, 2019. As of August 17, 2020:
https://www.mindanews.com/peace-process/2019/11/
northcot-turns-over-63-barangays-to-bangsamoro-region

Calungsod, Irish, "The Struggle of Finding One's Purpose: Omar's Story," *Peace Gazette*, No. 1, August 2019. As of August 17, 2020: https://gallery.mailchimp.com/b6ff4234bf3c5f1fb077d71d7/files/aba79690-d7ae-44fc-a9e0-bb411e8b9b4a/AUGUST_2019_STANDALONE.pdf

Carroll, Christopher, Malcolm Patterson, Stephen Wood, Andrew Booth, Jo Rick, and Shashi Balain, "A Conceptual Framework for Implementation Fidelity," *Implementation Science*, Vol. 2, No. 40, 2007.

"Cost of Living in Davao," *Numbeo*, webpage, undated. As of August 15, 2020: https://www.numbeo.com/cost-of-living/in/Davao

Dambi, Jermaine M., Lieselotte Corten, Matthew Chiwaridzo, Helen Jack, Tecla Mlambo, and Jennifer Jelsma, "A Systematic Review of the Psychometric Properties of the Cross-Cultural Translations and Adaptations of the Multidimensional Perceived Social Support Scale (MSPSS)," *Health and Quality of Life Outcomes*, Vol. 16, No. 1, 2018.

Dougherty, Cynthia M., Sandra K. Johnston, and Elaine Adams Thompson, "Reliability and Validity of the Self Efficacy Expectations and Outcome Expectations After ICD Implantation Scales," *Applied Nursing Research*, Vol. 20, No. 3, August 2007, pp. 116–124.

EdVenture Partners, "Past Success: Peer to Peer: Facebook Global Challenge," webpage, undated. As of July 21, 2020: https://www.edventurepartners.com/peer-to-peer-facebook-global-digital-challenge

Equal Access International, "About," webpage, undated a. As of August 12, 2020: https://www.equalaccess.org/about

———, "OURmindaNOW: Alternative Messaging Hub in Mindanao, Philippines," webpage, undated b. As of August 14, 2020: https://www.equalaccess.org/our-work/projects/alternative-messaging-hub-in-mindanao-philippines/

Facebook, "Peer to Peer (P2P): Facebook Global Digital Challenge," webpage, undated. As of August 12, 2020: https://counterspeech.fb.com/en/initiatives/p2p-facebook-global

Fouad, Nadya A., Philip L. Smith, and Larry Enochs, "Reliability and Validity Evidence for the Middle School Self-Efficacy Scale," *Measurement and Evaluation in Counseling and Development*, Vol. 30, No. 1, 1997, pp. 17–31.

Gayton, William F., Griffith R. Matthews, and Gregory N. Burchstead, "An Investigation of the Validity of the Physical Self-Efficacy Scale in Predicting Marathon Performance," *Perceptual and Motor Skills*, Vol. 63, No. 2, 1986, pp. 752–754.

Helmus, Todd C., and Elizabeth Bodine-Baron, *Empowering ISIS Opponents on Twitter*, Santa Monica, Calif.: RAND Corporation, PE-227-RC, 2017. As of August 11, 2020:
https://www.rand.org/pubs/perspectives/PE227.html

Hollingsworth, Julia, "Dramatic Images Show Impact of Deadly Earthquakes in Philippines," *CNN*, October 31, 2019. As of August 17, 2020:
https://www.cnn.com/2019/10/31/asia/philippines-earthquake-hotel-intl-hnk-scli/index.html

Jackson, Brian A., Ashley L. Rhoades, Jordan R. Reimer, Natasha Lander, Katherine Costello, and Sina Beaghley, *Practical Terrorism Prevention: Reexamining U.S. National Approaches to Addressing the Threat of Ideologically Motivated Violence*, Santa Monica, Calif.: RAND Corporation, RR-2647-DHS, 2019. As of August 21, 2020:
https://www.rand.org/pubs/research_reports/RR2647.html

"Magnitude 5.9 Quake Shakes Bukidnon, Part of Mindanao," *ABS-CBN News*, November 18, 2019. As of August 17, 2020:
https://news.abs-cbn.com/news/11/18/19/magnitude-59-quake-shakes-bukidnon-parts-of-mindanao

Marcellino, William M., Kim Cragin, Joshua Mendelsohn, Andrew Micahel Cady, Madeline Magnuson, and Kathleen Reedy, "Measuring the Popular Resonance of Daesh's Propaganda," *Journal of Strategic Security*, Vol. 10, No. 1, 2017, pp. 32–52.

Marrone, James V., Todd C. Helmus, Elizabeth Bodine-Baron, and Christopher Santucci, *Countering Violent Extremism in Nigeria: Using a Text-Message Survey to Assess Radio Programs*, Santa Monica, Calif.: RAND Corporation, RR-4257-DOS, 2020. As of August 17, 2020:
https://www.rand.org/pubs/research_reports/RR4257.html

OURmindaNOW, "Peace Promotion Fellows Undergo Experiential Learning Activity," webpage, undated. As of August 14, 2020:
https://ourmindanow.org/2020/02/14/peace-promotion-fellows-undergo-experiential-learning-activity

Philippine Statistics Authority, Region XI—Davao Region, "Factsheet on Islam in Mindanao," webpage, September 28, 2017. As of July 18, 2018:
http://rssol1.psa.gov.ph/article/factsheet-islam-mindanao

Reio, Thomas G., Jr., Tonette S. Rocco, Douglas H. Smith, and Elegance Chang, "A Critique of Kirkpatrick's Evaluation Model," *New Horizons in Adult Education and Human Resource Development*, Vol. 29, No. 2, Spring 2017, pp. 35–53.

Save the Children, "Facts and Figures: Philippines' Mindanao Island Earthquakes," webpage, undated. As of August 17, 2020:
https://www.savethechildren.org/us/what-we-do/emergency-response/philippines-earthquake-mindanao-island-2019-facts

Savoia, Elena, Max Su, Nigel Harriman, and Marcia A. Testa, "Evaluation of a School Campaign to Reduce Hatred," *Journal for Deradicalization*, No. 21, Winter 2019–2020.

Sobhani, Parinaz, Saif M. Mohammad, and Svetlana Kiritchenko, "Detecting Stance in Tweets and Analyzing Its Interaction with Sentiment," *Proceedings of the Fifth Joint Conference on Lexical and Computational Semantics*, Berlin, Germany, August 11–12, 2016, pp. 159–169.

"Social Media Statistics in the Philippines," *Talkwalker*, webpage, undated. As of August 12, 2020:
https://www.talkwalker.com/blog/social-media-statistics-philippines

Study of Terrorism and Responses to Terrorism Global Terrorism Database, data set, undated. As of August 12, 2020:
https://www.start.umd.edu/gtd

Villamor, Felipe, "As Mattis Arrives in the Philippines, Mop-Up in Marawi Is Declared Over," *New York Times*, October 23, 2017.

Weiss, Michael J., Howard Bloom, and Thomas Brock, "A Conceptual Framework for Studying the Sources of Variation in Program Effects," *Journal of Policy Analysis and Management*, Vol. 33, No. 4, 2014, pp. 1047–1049.

Zimet, Gregory D., Nancy W. Dahlem, Sara G. Zimet, and Gordon K. Farley, "The Multidimensional Scale of Perceived Social Support," *Journal of Personality Assessment*, Vol. 52, No. 1, 1988, pp. 30–41.